The Origins of the
Four Branches
of the Mabinogi

The Origins of the
Four Branches
of the Mabinogi

Andrew Breeze

GRACEWING

First published in 2009

Gracewing
2 Southern Avenue
Leominster
Herefordshire HR6 0QF

ISBN 978 0 85244 553 2

The picture of Gwenllian, by H. Williams, is reproduced with permission from the lithograph in the possession of Kidwelly Town Council.

Typeset by Action Publishing Technology Ltd, Gloucester GL1 5SR

Contents

Preface

The *Four Branches of the Mabinogi* are early Welsh tales of love, adventure, and magic. They form a group within the collection of eleven stories called the *Mabinogion*, and have normally been attributed to one unknown writer. This book discusses the date, provenance, and authorship of those four tales. It pays special attention to their presentation of character, point of view, and subject matter. From them it argues that their author was a woman, who can be identified on internal evidence as Gwenllian, a Gwynedd princess who married a prince of Dyfed, and who died fighting the Norman invader at Kidwelly in 1136.

When this hypothesis was first published in 1997, in chapter three of my *Medieval Welsh Literature*, it created a small international sensation, with articles in the British national press, BBC television interviews, and even a feature on Canadian radio. It has been cheering since then to see its ideas gaining ground. Yet the present book, where they are set out in detail, will still no doubt provoke controversy. It thus gives readers an interesting opportunity, now and in years to come, to sharpen their wits. They may decide whether its conclusions are likely to be true. Or (like some of my reviewers) they may think the status quo has it.

Some chapters of this book have already appeared in *Studi Medievali, Memoria y Civilización, Notes and Queries, Feilscribhínn Ghearóid Mhic Eoin,* and *Voprosy Filologii,* the last item being based on my lecture of 2003 to the Russian

Academy of Sciences, Moscow. I thank the editors of all these for allowing republication. I also thank Paul Russell for a copy of the chapter on place names; Professor Ian Kirby of Lausanne for taking on editorial duties that were holding up writing of the book; and Professor Herbert Richardson, for important advice on presentation of the arguments. I have special thanks for Count Tolstoy, who has long been generous in gifts of rare, useful, and interesting books on Celtic Studies, and characteristically courteous and honest in debate, even though his views on the *Four Branches* differ greatly from mine.

The bibliography was compiled in November 2004, when the book was finished, but I have added some references to items published since then. I regret not being able to include more.

I hope what follows will interest all those concerned with writing by women, especially in the Middle Ages. If Gwenllian was the author of the *Four Branches*, as the evidence suggests, she would be one of the great women writers of the world; perhaps the nearest thing to the female Shakespeare that Virginia Woolf dreamed of.

This book is dedicated to my wife Ruth, and to our children Patrick, Charles, Raffaella, Richard, James, and Anna.

AB

Did a Woman Write the *Four Branches of the Mabinogi*?

The role of women in the *Four Branches of the Mabinogi* has been considered on various occasions.[1] So, too, has the question of authorship.[2] Yet it seems never previously to have been noticed that the *Four Branches* show signs of having been written or composed by a woman. In what follows an attempt will be made, first, to prove that the *Four Branches* are the work of a woman, and, second, to show that she can be identified as Princess Gwenllian (*c*.1097–1136) of Gwynedd. Gwenllian was the daughter of Gruffudd ap Cynan, king of Gwynedd; the wife of Gruffydd ap Rhys, prince of Deheubarth (South Wales); and the mother of the Lord Rhys (d. 1197), who dominated the politics of West Wales in the later twelfth century.

If this identification is correct, we can date the *Four Branches* to between about 1120, when Gwenllian attained her majority, and 1136, when she was killed while leading an attack on the Norman garrison at Kidwelly, in South Wales. Other evidence suggests the *Four Branches* were actually composed in 1128 or slightly later. If Gwenllian did write the *Four Branches*, she almost certainly did so while living in the commote of Caio, between Lampeter and Llandovery in south-west Wales.

I

As we read the *Four Branches*, we again and again find passages which would be unusual if the work of a man, but which read naturally as the work of a woman. In the first branch, Pwyll takes on the form of Arawn, otherworld king of Annwn, and makes for his court. He arrives and is made welcome, sitting at table between Arawn's queen, 'the fairest woman any one had ever seen, dressed in a robe of shining gold brocaded silk', and the earl.[3] We hear more of the queen, 'the most unaffected woman, and the most gracious of disposition and discourse', and nothing of the earl. The writer was clearly interested in the queen, but had no interest in the earl. When Pwyll sleeps with the queen, he turns his back and retains his chastity over the entire year. After slaying Hafgan, Arawn's otherworld enemy, Pwyll meets Arawn, changes form and semblance with him, and returns home. Arawn comes back to his wife, goes to bed with her, and indulges in 'loving pleasure and affection'. She wonders at the apparent change in him. 'Alas, God,' said she, 'what different thought is there in him tonight from what has been since a year from tonight!' He is puzzled at her silence, and we hear their pillow talk. 'Shame on me', said she, 'if since a year from yesternight, from the time we were enfolded in the bedclothes, that there has been either delight or converse between us, or thou hast turned thy face towards me, let alone anything that would be more than that between us.' Arawn reflects on the steadfastness and unswerving fellowship of his comrade, and tells his wife all. 'By my confession to God,' said she, 'strong hold hadst thou on a comrade, for warding off fleshly temptation and for keeping faith with thee.' 'Lady,' said he, 'that was my thought too when I was silent with thee.' 'Nor was that strange', she replied.

The delicacy in thought and expression of this intimate passage has been noted. W. J. Gruffydd and others thought it showed the *Four Branches* were the work of a monk or other cleric.[4] But it reads more convincingly as the work of a woman. Arawn's wife gets the upper hand in the dialogue, where we have almost twice as many words from her as from him, and where she has the last word. We are also given an insight into her thoughts. This can be contrasted with the bedroom scenes in the Middle English poem *Sir Gawain and the Green Knight*, by a male author, where everything is seen from the point of view of Gawain, lying in bed, and not at all from the point of view of the lady of the castle, who enters his room secretly three mornings in a row to try and seduce him. The role given to Arawn's wife, her thoughts and feelings, would be less surprising if the passage were written by a woman.

In the next part of the story, Pwyll attempts to converse with a mysterious lady on a white horse, with a garment of shining gold brocaded silk about her, who passes the *gorsedd* or great mound at Arberth. No rider can overtake her, even Pwyll himself, until he asks her to stay for the sake of the one she loves best. It is she who commands the situation. She also commands the dialogue that follows. 'Lady,' he asked, 'whence comest thou, and where art thou going?' 'I go my own errands,' said she, 'and glad I am to see thee.' Her reply is both courteous and uninformative. But eventually she reveals that she is Rhiannon, and that she has come to see Pwyll because she is being given to another husband against her will. 'But no husband have I wished for, and that out of love of thee, nor will I have him even now unless thou reject me.' Pwyll comes up with the desired answer: 'If I had choice of all the ladies and maidens in the world, 'tis thou I would choose.' She bids him make a tryst; he agrees, and asks her to make it where she will; she tells him to come a year from that night to a feast she will have prepared at the court of Hefeydd the Old; he promises to come; and it is she who has the last word. 'Lord,' said she, 'fare thee well, and remember that thou keep thy promise, and I will go my way.' From beginning to end, it is Rhiannon who is in command. If this passage were written by a woman of character and high social rank, it would appear exactly as it does. But if it were written by a man, it would be curious that Pwyll is presented in it as so passive, even feeble. In this wooing, the shots are called by the woman, not the man.

The feast comes. Pwyll sits between Rhiannon and her father; a stranger enters, seeking a boon; and Pwyll promises him anything he wants, to Rhiannon's wiser comment, 'Alas, why does thou give such an answer?' The stranger is Rhiannon's unwanted suitor Gwawl, who asks for her. Dumbfounded, Pwyll knows not what to do. 'Be dumb as long as thou wilt', said Rhiannon. 'Never was there a man made feebler use of his wits than thou hast.' 'Lady,' said he, 'I knew not who he was.' Rhiannon bids Pwyll bestow her upon him, explaining, at his protests, that she will give him a small bag, and the feast to the warband and the retinues. She tells Pwyll to make a tryst a year from that night, as one of a hundred horsemen, and instructs him on all he must do to outwit Gwawl. When Gwawl demands an answer, it is Rhiannon who does the talking. Throughout this episode, it is Rhiannon who appears as a woman of authority and resource, used to making plans and ordering men about. Pwyll's authority and wits seem, in contrast, of a minor order. Rhiannon's 'Be dumb as long as thou wilt. Never was there a man made feebler use of his wits than thou hast' certainly shows scant respect for them. If this passage were written by a woman of high social rank, this would not be surprising; but if it were written by man, it would be difficult to explain why the supposed hero Pwyll is at a loss in a crisis, so oddly failing to live up to his own name (which means 'Sense').

This pattern continues when the feast comes a year later. It is Rhiannon who bids Gwawl tread down the bag of the disguised Pwyll, tells Pwyll the terms and sureties to demand after Gwawl is overcome, and the largesse to make minstrels and others on the following day. Rhiannon's own father, Hefeydd the Old, plays a minor role throughout (even, when he expects Pwyll to depart without his bride, a slightly ludicrous one, like a medieval Mr Woodhouse). On the arrival of Rhiannon and Pwyll at Arberth she again shows herself active, presenting each

written by a woman or standard folklore
motif? (woman of sovereignty)

man and woman of the court with 'a brooch or a ring or a precious stone'.

When a boy is born to Rhiannon, after a delay of over three years, we are given the famous episode in her bedroom, with her waiting women awaking at cockcrow to find the boy lost, becoming terrified of being burnt alive, and together devising the grotesque lie that she destroyed her own child. The author describes this incident in the women's quarters with a convincingness that might be thought remarkable for a male author. The pathos of the scene when Rhiannon, waking to find her child gone, pleads with the women to tell her the truth, likewise shows a power that would perhaps be surprising if a man had written it.

'"God who knows all things knows that accusation of me is false. And if it be fear that is upon you, by my confession to God I will protect you." "Faith," said they, "we will not bring hurt on ourselves for any one in the world." "Poor creatures," said she, "you will come to no hurt for telling the truth." For all her words, whether fair or pitiful, she got but the one answer from the women.'

Rhiannon is in no way at a loss in a crisis. But we see too her mingled sorrow, tenderness, generosity, and nobility. These qualities appear in her acceptance of her fate. She summons teachers and wise men, and, 'as she preferred doing penance to wrangling with the women, she took on her her penance'. Rhiannon's moral integrity is evident here, but we may also note the reference to her summoning of teachers and wise men. It is likely that Gwenllian as princess was accustomed to doing this. If the present hypothesis on authorship is correct, she may have done it in collecting material before dictating the *Four Branches*, which seem to have been written down at composition. As for Rhiannon's punishment, of sitting by a horseblock and carrying comers on her back, the author again shows delicacy in the comment, 'It was chance that anyone would permit himself to be carried.' In short, this part of the *Four Branches* shows Rhiannon as maintaining her dignity and moral authority, for all her grief, in prose that could hardly be improved. The author must also have been familiar with the speech and behaviour of women of the highest social rank.

When the narrative moves to Gwent, Teyrnon's battle with a night-monster outside his house is dealt with in summary fashion. ('Teyrnon drew his sword and struck off the arm at the elbow, so that that much of the arm together with the colt was inside with him.') Clearly, the author had no interest in monsters, fighting, or swords (unlike the author of *Beowulf*, which provides an analogue of this episode). But the writer was much interested in the baby that Teyrnon discovers and in the reaction of Teyrnon's wife to the lad. She is the third of the wives figuring in this branch and we hear much of her. She has no child, as Rhiannon for three years had no child. She asks about the silk garments on the baby, declares he is the son of gentlefolk, that it would be pleasure and mirth to her to bring him up, that she will bring women into league with her to do this (her husband readily agrees); we hear of the boy Gwri's baptism, hair, nursing, walking, growth, interest in horses, and his foster-mother's arrangements for him to be provided with horses (again, Teyrnon's role is to accord in this). When the boy is to be restored to Rhiannon, Teyrnon's wife gives her husband good advice; when the boy is handed over, we are told no person in the world will feel more grief than her for the loss of him (a trauma in part healed when agreement is made for the boy's fostering).

Teyrnon's wife is crucial for the conclusion drawn by this chapter. Arguments for female authorship of the *Four Branches* stand or fall by her. If a woman wrote the *Four Branches*, the prominent role given to Teyrnon's wife and her interest in a child are natural. On the other hand, if the *Four Branches* were the work of a man, his interest in such matters as childlessness, the provision of a wet nurse, or a foster-mother's sorrow on losing her child to another woman, would be unusual, to say the least.

what about a writer with a woman patron?

II

The second branch of the *Mabinogi* likewise deals with women and marriage, seen from a royal point of view. Matholwch, King of Ireland, comes with a fleet to ask for the hand of Branwen, sister of Bendigeidfran, King of Britain. When Branwen reaches Ireland, she bestows on nobles and ladies of the court 'a brooch or a ring or a treasured royal jewel, which it was a wondrous sight to see departing'. The last phrase, somewhat dry in tone, may suggest the author had personal experience of giving readily-accepted treasure to the Irish upper classes. After a year a son is born to Branwen, who is 'put out to foster in the very best place for men in Ireland'. But then follows the humiliation of Branwen in the king's kitchen, from which she escapes after three years by training a starling. Branwen instructed the starling, and brought it 'a letter of the woes and the dishonour that were upon her'. The bird flies with her message to Bendigeidfran at Caernarfon, where 'it alighted on his shoulder and ruffled its feathers so that the letter was seen and it was known that the bird had been reared among dwellings'. The casual reference to a letter, either written by Branwen herself, or written by another and appropriated by her as testimony of her plight, is remarkable evidence for women's consciousness of literacy at this date. Although the text does not say that Branwen wrote the letter, it shows the narrator's awareness of how a woman might use literacy to escape from bondage and male violence. That there is no actual mention of Branwen's writing the letter may suggest that the presumed woman author of the *Mabinogi* could not write. But it is a striking indication of the author's knowledge of written words, and of the power they could bring (in Branwen's case, a power that literally brings about her liberation).

This stratagem achieves redress for Branwen. Her brother at once prepares to invade Ireland to seek justice for her. When Branwen is addressed as 'Lady' to explain what is seen approaching across the Irish Sea, she begins with a wry 'Though lady I am not': both the response of a woman ill-treated by men, and a lady of high rank who, like Rhiannon with the waiting women, has been insulted by her social inferiors. Some commentators have seen Branwen as a slighter character than Rhiannon. This is no doubt true. Yet peace terms between Irish and Welsh are made 'by counsel of Branwen, and lest the land be laid waste she did that'. As a princess of Gwynedd, she is as capable of playing a part in Welsh-Irish politics and diplomacy as she is of organizing her own liberation from slavery. The kingship of Ireland is to be conferred on Gwern, Branwen's son, with 'all who saw him loving him'; but when Efnisien, in an act of madness, thrusts Gwern into the fire, Branwen makes as if to leap in too; yet Bendigeidfran saves her, and protects her in the fight that follows. Again, we hear almost nothing of the fight itself. The writer was not interested in describing it. But we do hear of a magic 'cauldron of rebirth', which restores life to slain Irishmen cast into it. The writer cares nothing for swords or spears, but is interested in this round womb-like entity, which is crucial to the plot. We need not subscribe to the theories of Sigmund Freud to see such emphasis as perhaps characteristic of a woman writer. When Branwen escapes to Britain with seven others, the author describes the pathos of her death.

'"Alas, Son of God!", said she. "Woe is me that ever I was born; two good islands have been laid waste because of me!" And she heaved a great sigh, and with that broke her heart. And a four-sided grave was made for her, and she was buried there on the bank of the Alaw.'

The tale ends with the curious anecdote of five pregnant women (the only people left alive in Ireland), and the description of the narrative as concerning the blow to Branwen, how it was avenged, the feasting at Harlech and Gwales, and the singing of the birds of Rhiannon.

III

Women play a less important role in the third branch than in the first, second, and fourth. Yet it begins with Pryderi's bestowal of his mother Rhiannon with the seven cantrefs of Dyfed on Bendigeidfran's brother, Manawydan. Pryderi tells Manawydan that, even after the eighty-seven years since the party left Ireland, he will not be ill-pleased with Rhiannon's looks. So it proves. On meeting her, Manawydan discovers he has never beheld a lady 'more graced with beauty and comeliness than she'. When Pryderi, his wife Cigfa, Manawydan, and Rhiannon are forced to live in exile in England, Manawydan seems to show wisdom in yielding to their foes, when Pryderi would reach for his sword. The four return to Dyfed. While hunting, Manawydan loses Pryderi inside a magic fortress. On his return, Rhiannon robustly tells him he is a bad comrade and has lost a good comrade, goes to find her son in the fortress, and is lost in a fall of mist. Cigfa, alone with Manawydan, fears for her virtue. He assures her of his honour. The tale ends with the ravaging by mice of Manawydan's lands. He captures one of them, pregnant, in his glove; she turns out to be the transformed wife of the magician Llwyd son of Cil Coed, who has been taking vengeance on Dyfed for the harm done to Gwawl in the first branch. By holding her hostage, Manawydan obtains the release of Pryderi and Rhiannon.

This tale provides a little more evidence for female authorship. The curious point about Rhiannon's looks and remarriage may be worth noting, since ageing is a subject on which women tend to be more sensitive than men ←w+f (hence the modern cosmetics industry). If the *Four Branches* were written by a woman, it may be no accident that fears for Rhiannon's beauty prove groundless, and she obtains a husband who is charmed by her. (Parallels here are the *Wife of Bath's Tale*, a middle-aged widow's story of a rejuvenated bride, and the novels of Jane Austen, described as the fantasies of an ageing spinster.) Cigfa's concern for her virtue is another subject more likely to worry a woman than a man, particularly in a traditional society; while Manawydan's desire to avoid conflict indicates the same regard for peacekeeping as is shown by Branwen in the second branch. Yet he later proves a coward, being humiliated by Rhiannon's scorn as she takes resolute action to recover her son: an episode certainly consistent with female authorship. Finally, even a plague of mice reveals that interest in pregnancy which is such a persistent feature of the *Four Branches*; a subject to which a woman author might relate.

IV

With the fourth branch we again find abundant material on women and children. Math, lord of Gwynedd, can live only with his feet in the fold of the lap of a virgin. At the beginning of the tale she is Goewin, daughter of Pebin. By tricking Pryderi, the magician Gwydion enables Math's nephew Gilfaethwy, who is in love with Goewin, to rape her. This incident is described with restraint. Gilfaethwy and Goewin 'were put to sleep together in Math son of Mathonwy's bed; and the maidens were roughly forced out, and she was lain with against her will that night'. When Math returns, Goewin protests to him, defending her virtue with the point, 'Nor did I bear it in quiet; there was none in the court did not know of it.' In medieval literature, concern of this kind for a woman's feelings in such an outrage is rare. Vengeance follows. Gilfaethwy and Gwydion are turned into animals, in successive years bearing offspring, transformed into boys who are respectively named Hyddwn, Hychdwn, and Bleiddwn. (The author is careful to tell us that Hychdwn was 'a fine boy with rich auburn hair'.) When Aranhod is called to take over Goewin's office, and has to step over a magic wand to test her virginity, she drops 'a fine boy-child with rich yellow hair', who is named Dylan, and a 'small something', which Gwydion hides in a chest at the foot of his bed.

When Gwydion wakes one morning, he hears a muffled

cry in the chest. He opens it to discover 'an infant boy thrusting his arms from the fold of the sheet and opening it apart.' Gwydion finds a wet nurse (a 'woman with breasts'), and we hear in some detail how the boy grew rapidly and how he loved Gwydion 'better than any one'. When the boy is four (attention to children's ages is a feature of these tales), Aranrhod discovers who he is and curses him. He shall get no name, unless from her; he shall bear no arms, unless she equip him; he shall have no wife of the race now on earth. The first of these curses is of interest. There is repeated emphasis in the *Four Branches* on children's baptism, described (somewhat artlessly) as the baptism 'which they used in those days'. Robert Thomson notes that for the author, as for many people today, the important thing about baptism was the name-giving (not the infusion of supernatural grace).[5] A child's baptism, considered as name-giving, is perhaps a concern of mothers rather than fathers. To deny a child a name might thus seem especially unnatural to a female author. Aranrhod here commits something close to child abuse and the author condemns her for it.

These curses Gwydion overcomes by magic. When the boy, named Lleu Llaw Gyffes, is 'a man in stature, and the handsomest youth that mortal ever saw', Gwydion circumvents the last curse by making him a bride from flowers, who is named Blodeuedd. But she is unfaithful to her husband, taking the initiative in the affair with her lover, Gronw. With her husband absent, it is she who invites the hunter Gronw into her court; she comes herself to meet him and welcome him; they change their clothes and sit down. Then,

> Blodeuedd looked on him, and the moment she looked there was no part of her that was not filled with love for him. And he too gazed on her, and the same thought came to him as had come to her. He might not conceal that he loved her, and he told her so. She knew great joy at heart, and their talk that night was of the affection and love they had conceived one for the another. Nor did they delay longer than that night ere they embraced each other. And that night they slept together.

We are told how she loved him before we hear how he loved her; we hear of her feelings for him, rather than his for her; the attention is on her, not him. She continues to take the initiative throughout the affair. When Gronw tries to leave the next day, she holds him back, declaring, 'Faith, thou wilt not go from me tonight.' The day after she again prevents him from leaving, keeping him for a third night. She is the dominant partner of the two. Together, Blodeuedd and Gronw attempt to murder Lleu. The tale ends when, through Gwydion's efforts, Gronw is killed and Blodeuedd transformed into an owl. Lleu, restored to his normal form, rules as lord of Gwynedd.

The fourth branch provides varied evidence for female authorship. It is striking that, although rape and adultery are central parts of the plot, they are described with restraint. Babies likewise figure largely, above all the infant Lleu. The account of the baby crying in a chest, waving his hands in the air, and being found a 'woman with breasts' to nurse him, might have been written by a man (though it is not easy to think of a similar passage written by one), but reads more naturally as the work of a woman. So does the narrative of Blodeuedd's affair with Gronw. It is written from the woman's point of view; it is her seduction of him, rather than his of her. If a woman composed the *Four Branches*, she might naturally describe a love affair as seen and promoted by the woman. But, if a man wrote the account of the love of Gronw and Blodeuedd, Gronw's somewhat passive role in it is hard to explain. We can go further. Although Aranrhod and Blodeuedd are formidable women, they are overcome by a male character, Gwydion. Yet this need not indicate a male author, because Aranrhod is a bad mother, Blodeuedd a bad wife. That they fail in their wickedness shows the author condemning cruelty to children and adultery as the evils they are. This attitude may be more typical of a female writer than a male one. It would be especially so of a married female writer with children.

V

The evidence set out above for the *Four Branches* as the work of a woman writer is of a cumulative nature. There are male writers who have disliked describing fighting and weapons, and who have given an important place to women and children (to say nothing of fine clothes and jewels) in their work. An obvious example of this is Chaucer. Yet even he has been typified by Derek Pearsall as having a view of women that is far from escaping medieval male stereotypes. Pearsall has a pertinent comment here on Chaucer's representation of women's sexuality. Here Chaucer, 'like other medieval male writers, finds himself both repelled and fascinated. Women must be idealized or deliberately made disgusting'.[6] Yet neither attitude occurs in the *Four Branches*. Sleeping together is seen as the normal end of courtship, as with Rhiannon and Branwen; with Arawn's wife, the act of love is seen as totally normal; Blodeuedd and Gronw's falling in love is also seen as a normal process, neither idealized nor (despite its evil consequences) made out as disgusting. So the author of the *Four Branches* has a viewpoint very different from the medieval male writers cited by Pearsall; especially clerical writers. This point must create difficulties for critics with much to say on the mysogyny of medieval clerics, who would at the same time have us believe that the *Four Branches* are the work of a monk or priest.

If critics insist on seeing the *Four Branches* as written by a man, certain features beside the above must seem unusual. The first is the repeated dominant role of women (who sometimes treat their males as inferiors), and the weakness or passivity of some male characters (variously seen in Pwyll, Teyrnon, Matholwch, Manawydan, Gilfaethwy, Gronw, and Lleu). The women characters of women writers tend to be more convincing than their male characters, and the *Four Branches* seem to bear this out. In this context one may recall Dickens's conclusion, in one of his letters, that 'George Eliot' was surely a woman writer, since in her first pseudonymous novel *Scenes from Clerical Life* the female characters are better drawn than the male ones; matters are repeatedly seen from a woman's point of view, as in the break-up of a love affair; and there is consistent interest in children, including a description of a woman mending children's clothes.[7] (Compare, more pungently, another critic's remark that he could think of no male character in a novel by a woman who was not, in the end, a booby. There are boobyish aspects of many men in the *Four Branches*; though significantly not of Bendigeidfran, for reasons discussed below.)

Secondly, after the dominant role of women, one may note the delicacy (almost 'chastity') in narrating the relations of men and women, as seen in the first, third, and fourth branches. For some this has suggested a clerical author.[8] But this opinion is difficult to reconcile with, for example, the intimate account of how Blodeuedd fell in love with Gronw. This does not read like the work of a cleric, but of a woman who knows what falling in love is like.

Third is the repeated interest in motherhood and babies (even extending to their appearance and need for milk). Childlessness, loss of a new-born baby, the grief of a foster-mother on losing her child to another woman: these are matters in the *Four Branches* rarely touched on by male writers, but of natural interest to a woman. Fourth is the author's lack of interest in bloodshed and warfare. This contrasts sharply with accounts of swords, spears, combat, and sudden death in literature from Homer onwards, and featuring in English writing from *Beowulf* to Malory. However, one may note that the author, though indifferent to combat and military hardware, was intimately concerned with the organizational and diplomatic aspects of war, as also its human tragedy. This is evident from the aftermath of Bendigeidfran's invasion of Ireland in the second branch, and the fate of Pryderi's attack on Gwynedd in the fourth. Here it forms an aspect of the author's understanding of government and politics, which has been given particular recognition in recent years by

Catherine McKenna and Brynley Roberts, amongst others.[9]

On the basis of all this, it seems reasonable to see the *Four Branches* as the work of a woman writer. There is nothing impossible in this. That women could write vernacular literature at this date is shown by Marie de France, a poetess (possibly of royal blood) of the later twelfth century, whose work includes love and babies amongst its subjects. There is an even more striking parallel to the *Four Branches* in medieval Japanese, in *The Tale of Genji* (a point made to the present writer by Professor Fergus Kelly of Dublin). This was composed by Murasaki Shikibu (*c*.980–*c*.1030), a married lady and mother in the service of the Empress Akiko. Although Genji's adventures are all amorous, the narrative is of great charm 'and not at all indecent'. Fighting has little place in it, but we hear much of babies and children. Because *The Tale of Genji* was certainly composed by a woman, it provides a valuable check for analysis of the *Four Branches*.

None of these arguments look at women of the place relevant - comparisons are of other countries and/or times

VI

If the *Four Branches* are actually the work of a woman writer, can we go farther and say who she was? It seems we can. There are strong grounds for taking the author as Gwenllian, daughter of Gruffudd ap Cynan. Her authorship would explain many features of the text.

Gwenllian was the daughter of Gruffudd ap Cynan (*c*.1055–1137), king of Gwynedd; her mother was Angharad, daughter of Owain ab Edwin (a descendant of Hywel Dda). Gruffudd, subject of a unique Middle Welsh biography, married his wife about 1095, after long exile in Ireland. Gwenllian, who had three brothers, was the oldest of five sisters. Although we cannot know exactly what she looked like, by an extraordinary chance we do have a description of her mother, said to be 'of noble birth, well-grown, with fair hair, large-eyed, of fine shape, with queenly figure and strong limbs and well-made legs and the best of feet, and long fingers and thin nails; kindly and eloquent, and good at food and drink; wise and prudent, a woman of good counsel, merciful towards her kingdom, charitable to the needy, and just in all things'.[10] Even if we discount a conventional element, it is likely the daughter took after the mother in looks and physique. Perhaps the descriptions of the mother as 'eloquent', 'good at food and drink', 'of good counsel', 'merciful towards her kingdom', and 'just in all things' also deserve consideration here. All these qualities may be exemplified in the *Mabinogi*, particularly 'eloquence', though many recent scholars have noted as well a concern with wise and just government, one Canadian scholar even calling it a 'mirror for princes'.[11] ('Handbook for politicians' might equally well express its political realism on the practical settlement of disputes.)

There is in any case good reason to believe that Gwenllian possessed courage and resource, as well as beauty and good health. Shortly after 1116, when she was nineteen, Gwenllian married Gruffydd ap Rhys (*c.*1090–1137), prince of Deheubarth (South Wales), who had been an exile in Ireland from early childhood until his return to Dyfed in 1113. After many hazards, including full-scale rebellion against Henry I in 1116, Gruffydd lived quietly (except for a brief Irish exile in 1127) in the commote of Caio (between Lampeter and Llandovery, within the three cantrefs of Ystrad Tywi mentioned at the close of the first branch and beginning of the fourth). Gruffydd's sons by Gwenllian were Maredudd, Rhys (1132–97), Morgan, and Maelgwn. The second is famous as the 'Lord Rhys', founder of Talley Abbey, and effective founder of Strata Florida. Anarawd (murdered in 1143) and Cadell (who died at Strata Florida in 1175, after an eventful life) were Gruffydd's sons by an earlier union.

Gwenllian died very early in 1136, beheaded after Maurice of London routed an attack led by her with her sons Morgan (also killed) and Maelgwn (taken prisoner) against Kidwelly. Writing of the battle over fifty years later, Gerald of Wales described Gwenllian as riding forward 'at the head of an army, like some Penthesilea,

Queen of the Amazons'. The battlefield (now in state care) north of Kidwelly is still called *Maes Gwenllian* 'Gwenllian's Field'.[12] There is no doubt of the strong impression Gwenllian made in her time.

VII

Even if we accept that the *Four Branches* were written by a woman, what reason have we to believe she may have been Princess Gwenllian? The evidence is circumstancial, but nothing in it suggests she could not have been. It is worth emphasizing here, first, that if Gwenllian did not write the *Four Branches*, there should be clear evidence against her authorship (but there seems none); and, second, that the case for her authorship tallies with the information provided by the text even in small details. We can drawn an analogy from a modern law court. Experienced lawyers there place high value on the details of evidence (the notes in a policeman's notebook, and so on) for corroboration. The importance of circumstantial evidence should also be noted. Almost all scientific evidence given in a courtroom, including that of ballistics experts, is circumstantial. One's fingerprints on a murder weapon, traces of one's DNA on clothing at a crime scene, are also circumstantial, but have hanged men nonetheless. So the circumstantial information provided by the *Four Branches* may suggest to thoughtful readers a verdict for Gwenllian's authorship. It may be set out as follows:

1. Once we admit an early medieval literary text to be the work of a woman, we limit the number of potential authors. Only a woman of high rank would be in a position to write such a text or have it copied; only if she were within an influential circle would copies of it continue to be made. As mother of the Lord Rhys, a protector of monasteries and patron of bards, Gwenllian would be well placed for her writings to survive after her time.

2. The author of the *Four Branches* had an intimate knowledge of the courts of kings and princes, and a royal attitude to life. Women like Rhiannon organize their lives with confidence; even Branwen possesses political skills. In matters of social inferiors, such as Rhiannon's treatment by the waiting women or Branwen's by the butcher, we see things from the princess's point of view. If a princess wrote the *Four Branches*, this would not be surprising.

3. The author had a detailed knowledge of Gwynedd, a less detailed one of Dyfed, and a shadowy one of Gwent and the rest of Britain. The author even knows of Gronw's stone, just over five foot long, and still to be seen a mile from Ffestiniog.[13] As regards Dyfed, the region really known well is the Teifi valley, which forms the northern border of Caio, where Gwenllian lived. W. J. Gruffydd suggested the 'Arberth' of the first branch was in north Pembrokeshire, near Glyn Cuch and the Preseli Mountains, which are also mentioned.[14] But Professor R. Geraint Gruffydd of Aberystwyth informs the present writer that Arberth is in Ceredigion, in the parish of Llangoedmor, about a mile east of Cardigan. In the same parish is the conspicuous hill of Crug Mawr, where, some months after Gwenllian's death, her husband defeated the Normans (probably on 10 October 1136). Lloyd describes it as a knoll, now called 'Banc y Warren', two miles outside Cardigan on the road to Aberystwyth. As *Cruc maur* in *Cereticiaun* it is one of the *mirabilia* of *Historia Brittonum*. This suggests it was the magic *gorsedd* or mound from which Pwyll first saw Rhiannon.[15] In any case, both Dyfed and Gwynedd are praised in the *Four Branches*. At the start of the third branch, Pryderi says there are no finer cantrefs than the seven cantrefs of Dyfed; in the fourth branch, Math describes the cantref of Dinoding (around the north-eastern corner of Cardigan Bay) as 'the very best cantref for a young man to have'.[16] The defeat in the fourth branch of a Dyfed army by one of Gwynedd is also described with tact.

Such knowledge and praise of Gwynedd and Dyfed would not be surprising if the *Four Branches* were written by Gwenllian, a Gwynedd princess married to a Dyfed prince. The Dyfed dialect of the manuscripts (if Gwenllian did not acquire it) would be due to her scribe or to later copyists.

4. The knowledge of Ireland shown in the *Four Branches* accords with the exile there of Gwenllian's father and husband. Their circumstances of involuntary exile may account for the second branch's somewhat negative view of the Irish. Branwen's position in Ireland also parallels that of Gwenllian in Dyfed. Through marriage, each was living away from her immediate kin. Both had powerful kinsmen who were rulers of Gwynedd. Derick Thomson has related the divided loyalties of Branwen to women of the age and circle of Gruffudd ap Cynan.[17] If Gwenllian wrote the *Four Branches*, his point is more apt than he thinks. Branwen's vindication with the arrival of her brother's fleet in Ireland would be a comforting passage for Gwenllian to write. Like Bendigeidfran, Gruffudd organized an invasion by sea (in 1081, when he landed Welsh, Irish, and Viking troops near St Davids). In 1138 Gwenllian's stepsons Anarawd and Cadell brought over fifteen Viking ships (probably from Dublin) to attack Cardigan castle.[18] For the men of action who were Gwenllian's kin, organizing naval assaults in the Irish Sea was no mere literary motif. As regards the dating of the *Four Branches*, it is worth noting that Gruffydd ap Rhys was briefly exiled to Ireland in 1127. Presumably he went to Dublin, presumably with his wife. If so, it is possible Gwenllian composed the *Four Branches* on their return to Wales. The second branch tells how the Irish broke down a bridge over the 'Llinon' or Liffey.[19] This must allude to the bridge built in Dublin about the year 1000 at the foot of the modern Bridge Street, on the site of the present Father Mathew Bridge.[20] The possibility that Gwenllian wrote the *Four Branches* after exile in

Ireland in 1127 accords with the belief that so great a work of art is more likely to be by a woman of about thirty, with experience of life's vicissitudes, than by a young wife in her early twenties.

5. The *Four Branches* emphasize royal descent and status. The first branch begins with a statement of Pwyll's princely rank; the second, with one of Bendigeidfran's exaltation with the crown of London (an expression making sense only after 1066. The Confessor was crowned on Easter Day 1043 at Winchester. But Harold, the Conqueror, William Rufus, and Henry I were all crowned at Westminster). Such references would be natural for Gwenllian, daughter of a king, wife of a prince. We could even see the character of Bendigeidfran as reflecting Gwenllian's own memories of her father, in assembly at Caernarfon or on campaign. The knowledge of law in the *Four Branches*, especially on such matters as horses or honour-price, is also consistent with princely authorship. What we do not find is evidence for bookish Latin learning. There are no allusions to the Bible, or to Cicero or Vergil (in contrast to *Historia Gruffud vab Kenan*, certainly by a cleric).[21] We hear much of royal courts: nothing suggests the cloister. With a total lack of allusion to such religious centres as St Davids or Llanbadarn, this must (*pace* the memory of Proinsias Mac Cana) count against his attempt to link the *Four Branches* with the circle of Bishop Sulien (d. 1081) and his son Rhygyfarch.[22] Nor does anything suggest the influence of Geoffrey of Monmouth, whose *History of the Kings of Britain* was published after Gwenllian's death.

6. Jackson and others have noted the *Four Branches* are hardly the work of a professional storyteller, but of 'antiquarian literary men' whose writing is 'the product of the study rather than the mead-hall'.[23] This account (where Jackson apparently makes out the author of the *Four Branches* to be someone rather like himself) can be modified in the light of the evidence

A prof. storyteller could have difficulty from spoken to written though for Gwenllian's possible authorship of the tales. Although in no way a professional storyteller, she might yet be the kind of person capable of reworking half-forgotten tales into language 'masterly for its ease, refinement, and limpidity'. Jackson also notes the author's easy familiarity with the ceremonies and luxuries of court life. Again, the familiarity is more likely to be the attribute of a princess than of antiquarian scholars.

7. The royal houses of Gwynedd and Dyfed were known for literary interests. The Latin life of Gruffudd ap Cynan, written soon after his death (but known only from a later Welsh translation), is one aspect of this. Another is the poetry of Hywel (d. 1170), son of Gwenllian's brother Owain. Hywel's poems figure in *The Oxford Book of Welsh Verse*. If the *Four Branches* were by his aunt, it would accord with the family's talents. (We discuss below links between the language of the *Four Branches* and of Hywel's poems.) These literary interests were continued by Gwenllia'ns son, the Lord Rhys, who instigated the Cardigan eisteddfod of 1176.[24] Gwenllian's grandnephew also had literary interests. He was none other than Gerald of Wales, grandson of Princess Nest, sister of Gwenllian's husband Gruffydd. Although not closely related to Gwenllian by blood, he yet shows the unexpected links between writers and royalty in Wales at this date.

8. Gwenllian was married to a Deheubarth prince somewhat down on his luck, living in reduced circumstances in the hills of Caio; and a strong note of Dyfed irredentism runs though the *Four Branches*. The first branch opens by describing Pwyll as Prince of Dyfed. *Math* opens by describing Pryderi son of Pwyll as lord over one-and-twenty cantrefs of the South: the seven cantrefs of Dyfed, the seven of Glamorgan, the four of Ceredigion, and the three of Ystrad Tywi. The *Four Branches* look back to the ancient glories of the realm of Deheubarth, an attempt to revive which led to

Gwenllian's execution at Kidwelly in 1136. Her
commitment to the cause of a greater Dyfed tallies
with the political implications of the *Four Branches*. In
the light of this, it is difficult to accept Mac Cana's
suggestion that the *Four Branches* were written by a
Gwent man.[25] Had they been, their political geography would surely be different. Nor would they show
such intimate knowledge of places in Dyfed and
Gwynedd.

9. Gwenllian's life coincides with the period to which
the *Four Branches* is normally dated (between 1050 and
1120). Yet Sims-Williams, demolishing attempts to
give more precise dating to them, has with justice
quoted Mac Cana's view that the dating is 'still very
much an open question'.[26] If in attributing the *Four
Branches* to Gwenllian we date them to 1128 or slightly
later, this does not strain such other evidence for
dating as the relative paucity of loanwords in the tales
(*pali* 'brocaded silk', *cordwal* 'Cordovan leather', *swmer*
'sumpter', of which the first only must be directly
from French).

10. Gwenllian was a contemporary of 'Bledhericus Late-
meri' (*sic*), active in the Carmarthen region from 1089
until his death in about 1133. We hear much of him.
The son of Cadifor of Dyfed (d. 1089), he defended in
1116 the castle of Robert Courtemain against
Gruffydd ap Rhys. At a date between 1129 and 1133
he gave land to Carmarthen Priory. He may be Bledri
'the well-known storyteller, who lived a little before
our time' mentioned by Gerald of Wales (1146–1223),
and the Welshman called Bleheris who (according to
the second continuator of the *Conte del Graal*) told the
story of Perceval to William, count of Poitou from
1086 to 1127.

What matters for our purposes is that Thomas,
Anglo-Norman author of *Tristan*, refers to a certain
'Breri' as his authority for the poem and names
Iseult's female companion as 'Brangien'. This 'Brang-
ien' probably derives from 'Branwen'. If Thomas's

source for the name was Bledhericus, who knew the tale of Branwen as told by his neighbour Gwenllian (Caio is some twenty miles from Carmarthen), this would explain how a name which is rare in any written source reached the French poet.[27] It would also give the *Four Branches* a *terminus ad quem* of about 1133, when Bledhericus died. Since it is unlikely he learned the tale of Branwen on his deathbed, this strengthens the case for dating the *Four Branches* to 1128 or slightly later.

11. The hypothesis of Gwenllian's authorship of the *Four Branches* is supported by the provenance of the MS Peniarth 6 fragments of the second and third branch, and of the later White Book of Rhydderch. In a letter of 18 January 1995, Dr Daniel Huws (formerly of the National Library of Wales) told the writer that the standard dating of the fragments to about 1225 was some fifty years too early, and that their script most closely resembled that of the Hendregadredd Manuscript, of about 1300. That manuscript was written at the Cistercian abbey of Strata Florida, effectively the creation of Gwenllian's son, the Lord Rhys. It was the burial ground of his descendants, including his grandson Maredudd ab Owain (d. 1265), whose children Efa and Gruffudd were literary patrons. The links between Gwenllian's descendants and the manuscripts can be expressed as follows. The Peniarth 6 fragments can be associated with the Hendregadredd Manuscript, begun probably at Strata Florida about 1300; Strata Florida was strongly associated with Gwenllian's descendants; the third part of the Hendregadredd Manuscript was written some ten miles from Strata Florida at the home of Ieuan Llwyd, a descendant of Gwenllian via Maredudd ab Owain, who was Ieuan's great-great-grandfather; and the White Book of Rhydderch, written in about 1330 for Ieuan's son Rhydderch, contains Welsh translations (commissioned by Maredudd's son Gruffudd) of *Transitus Mariae* and pseudo-Turpin's history of

Charlemagne, as also a translation (commissioned by Maredudd's daughter Efa) of the Athanasian Creed.[28] If the *Four Branches* were by Gwenllian, their appearance in manuscripts associated with her descendants should cause no surprise.

12. A further test for Gwenllian's authorship of the *Four Branches* comes from poems by her nephew, Hywel (d. 1170) ab Owain Gwynedd. If the *Four Branches* were the work of Hywel's aunt, they should parallel his poems in grammar, vocabulary, and syntax. This is certainly true as regards vocabulary. Here the *Four Branches* and Hywel's poems, written in lucid upper-class Middle Welsh, are effectively identical. Some of their characteristic formations are not uncommon, like *duüno* 'agree', and *gosteg* 'silence'. But they also share words or formations which may be found elsewhere in poetry or prose, but are rarely found in both. Examples are *hyweddu* 'to tame', *marannedd* 'treasure', *dihenydd* 'execution', *pall* 'tent', *brawdfaeth* 'foster-brother', *taeru* 'maintain', *gorawenus* 'joyous', *parabl* 'utterance', and *pali* 'brocaded silk'. Two instances deserve special mention. In a love poem, Hywel describes a girl as

> Mabinaidd, luniaidd, lawn gweddeiddrwydd,
> Mabddysg oedd iddi rhoddi yn rhwydd.
> Mabwraig, mwy yd ffaig ffenedigrwydd ar wen
> Na pharabl o'i phen anghymhenrwydd.
> Peddestrig iolydd a'm bydd eilwydd,
> Pa hyd y'th iolaf? Saf rhag dy swydd.

That is,

> Child-like, well-formed, full of comeliness,
> Young she was trained to be bountiful;
> Young woman, more passion will come to the fair
> Than unseemly speech from her lips.
> Pacing, pleading, shall I have a tryst?
> How long must I ask you? Come meet me![29]

There is a possible link between *mabinogi* and the unique verbal sequence *mabinaidd, mabddysg, mabwraig. Peddestrig* 'walking' is also rare. Hywel's use of it curiously resembles that in the first branch. Pwyll's servant followed Rhiannon 'as fast as he could on foot (*o pedestric*), but the greater was his speed, all the further was she from him.' He tries again on horseback, but 'his horse flagged, and when he knew of his horse that its speed (*y bedestric*) was failing, he returned to where Pwyll was'. In using *peddestrig*, Hywel seems to be comparing himself to Pwyll's servant, who can do nothing unless the lady change her mind. Hywel's unique reference to *tonn Dylan* is also closely paralleled in the name *Dylan Eil Ton* 'Dylan son of Wave' in the fourth branch.[30] The similarity of vocabulary between the *Four Branches* and Hywel's poems accords with the proposition that they are the work of aunt and nephew. They also resemble each other in the intimate love they show of the landscape of Gwynedd, and, perhaps, their frank recognition of the love of man and woman.

13. Irish literature may also help date the *Four Branches*. It has long been recognized that one source of *Branwen* is *Mesca Ulad* 'The Intoxication of the Ulstermen' as contained in the Book of Leinster. That text has been dated to within fairly close limits. Thurneysen argued on stylistic grounds that it had the same redactor as the Book of Leinster *Táin*, who was also the author of *Cath Ruis na Ríg* 'The Battle of Rosnaree'. Thurneysen dated the career of this man, his 'Bearbeiter C', to the first third, perhaps the first quarter, of the twelfth century.[31]

If the *Four Branches* show knowledge of the work of Bearbeiter C, they must postdate him. Given the lapse of time needed for a Welsh writer to come across an Irish text, this would suggest *Four Branches* hardly predate the second or third decade of the twelfth century. We may note that this evidence for dating the *Four Branches* is independent of arguments for attributing them to Gwenllian; but it nevertheless tallies neatly with the date of soon after 1127 suggested above, when Gwenllian's husband is known to have been in Ireland. Perhaps Gwenllian came across *Mesca Ulad* while in Dublin. It is certainly a Leinster text. Derick Thomson's valuable discussion of the relation of *Mesca Ulad* to the second branch is unfortunately spoiled by his belief that *Mesca Ulad* is no older than the Book of Leinster itself, of about 1160. Knowing the *Four Branches* to be earlier than 1160, he is therefore forced to suggest the Iron House story of the second branch is an interpolation.[32] But, once we recognized the Book of Leinster *Mesca Ulad* as of the earlier twelfth century, the need for this argument vanishes.

Gwenllian's proposed authorship of the *Four Branches* also has an implication for Bearbeiter C. If she postdates him, he must predate her. Dating the *Four Branches* to 1128 or slightly later would therefore vindicate Thurneysen's placing of Bearbeiter C in the first third, or even first quarter, of the twelfth century. It is true that Thurneysen's arguments here have been criticized, with some reason, by O'Rahilly and Mac Eoin.[33] Nevertheless, if Gwenllian wrote the *Four Branches* using the work of Bearbeiter C, Thurneysen's conclusions must be substantially correct. Her authorship must also be fatal to Ó Concheanainn's belief that Bearbeiter C was none other than Áed Mac Crimthainn, the scribe-compiler of the Book of Leinster in the later twelfth century.[34]

14) The last main argument for Gwenllian's authorship of the *Four Branches* derives from their geographical orientation. Their view of Welsh geography accords well with what we should expect of a Gwynedd writer living in the commote of Caio at a time when south Dyfed was occupied by the Normans. The Teifi valley, which forms the northern border of the commote, is crucial here. In its lower basin are Arberth, the northern slopes of the Preseli Mountains, and Glyn Cuch,

which are discussed above. Upstream was Pryderi's court at Rhuddlan Teifi, near Llandysul in south Ceredigion. About 1165 Gwenllian's own son, the Lord Rhys, gave it and its 'rich meadows' to the monks of Whitland.[35] If Rhys's mother wrote the *Four Branches*, we could see the place as one with special significance for both of them. When Gwydion steals Pryderi's swine, he escapes via Mochdref 'in the uplands of Ceredigion' (that is, Nant-y-Moch, above the 1000–foot contour on the western slopes of Plynlimon), before moving eastwards into Powys.[36] The easiest route for him to take would be up the Teifi valley, moving swine in haste via Lampeter and then Devil's Bridge, which would take him immediately past Gwenllian's husband's domain of Caio. The reference to Hereford in the third branch also fits in with the hypothesis that the *Four Branches* were composed at Caio. Hereford is easily reached from Caio by the ancient road though Brecon and Hay-on-Wye. So it may be no coincidence that Manawydan and his companions are stated as carrying out their trade in Hereford (relatively accessible from Caio), rather than (say) Bristol, Shrewsbury, or Chester, which are farther away.

In addition to the above, there are five lesser arguments for Gwenllian's authorship of the *Four Branches*. Though not conclusive, they provide corroboration for the fourteen arguments above.

15. It seems another of Gwenllian's descendants, via Ednyfed Fychan of Gwynedd, was the poet Dafydd ap Gwilym.[37] Hence it may be that the greatest of Welsh poets descended from the greatest of Welsh prose writers. Dafydd's fondness for alluding to the *Four Branches*, rather than to other prose narratives accessible to him, has often been noted.[38] Perhaps he knew an ancestor of his was their author. Welsh royalists and others may also be cheered to learn that HRH the Prince of Wales is likewise a descendant of Gwenllian, through Ednyfed Fychan (d. 1246) and Henry VII.

16. The fourth branch closes with a puzzling allusion to the 'Three Disloyal Warbands'. A triad explains these as the warbands of Goronwy, of Gwrgi and Peredur, and of Alan Fyrgan. The last was a real person: Alan IV (d. 1119), Duke of Brittany, son-in-law of William the Conqueror, and ally of Henry I. Alan's son was Brian fitz Count (*fl.* 1119–42), lord of Abergavenny, who in Gwenllian's time was living less than forty miles from the border of Caio.[39] This circumstance may add to the case for dating the *Four Branches* after 1119, when a gibe against Alan, father of a local alien ruler, would have more bite. It also accords with the case for attributing the *Four Branches* to Brian's neighbour in South Wales, Gwenllian.

17. A fundamental aspect of the *Four Branches*, as of Welsh literature as a whole (even in the twenty-first century), is that of the unity of Britain, shattered when sovereignty was lost to a foreign invader.[40] Towards the end of the second branch, Manawydan learns that Caswallon son of Beli has conquered the Isle of the Mighty and is a crowned king in London. For what it is worth, the politics of this accords well with the later part of Henry I's reign, when the English crown had a tight grip on Wales, rather than with (for example) the reign of Stephen, a period of anarchy fully exploited by the Welsh. If Gwenllian wrote the *Four Branches*, it would not be too much to see the pessimism of this passage as reflecting a defeatist mentality amongst the Welsh in the period before Henry I's death in 1135.

18. In the third branch, Pryderi goes to Caswallawn in Oxford and tenders him homage. This reference to Oxford is surprising, since the town was under a cloud until well into the twelfth century. The first sign of its new importance came with the building of the King's House, on a site north-east of the modern Worcester College. A royal charter of 1133, 'when the king visited his new house, is the first evidence of a royal presence in the town for nearly seventy years'.[41] If we take this at face value and assume Pryderi's act

of allegiance reflects the events of 1133, this creates some difficulty for the dating proposed above of the *Four Branches* to 1128 or slightly later, and certainly before about 1133, when Bledhericus died. However, it is surely the case that Henry I was in Oxford for the purpose of government before 1133, and that evidence may be brought forward to prove this. Oxford was conveniently near his hunting-lodge at Woodstock (mentioned in the *Anglo-Saxon Chronicle* for 1123, which tells how the Bishop of Lincoln collapsed and died there). The King's House would not have been built unless Henry had found growing business in Oxford made a base there necessary. If so, the *Four Branches* would reflect Henry I's visits to Oxford in the 1120s and early 1130s. It is not easy otherwise to see why Oxford, which plays no great part in medieval Welsh tradition, should figure in the *Four Branches*.[42] Alternatively, 'Oxford' might be the author's short-hand for 'Woodstock'. The distinction between the two would mean little when seen from Wales. Henry I's interest in Oxford in no way damages the case for attributing the *Four Branches* to Gwenllian; who would have more than usual concern with Henry, since her sister-in-law Nest (who long outlived her) was one of his lovers.

19. Although the *Four Branches* deal mainly with Gwynedd and Dyfed, Glamorgan also has a place in their political geography. At the opening of the fourth branch the seven cantrefs of Morgannwg are amongst Pryderi's domains, part of the historic realm of Deheubarth. It may be no coincidence that two of Gwenllian's stepdaughters were married to Glamorgan rulers. Gwladus was married to Caradog ab Iestyn (active in 1127), Nest to Ifor Bach of Senghenydd (who made a sensational raid on Cardiff Castle in 1158). Caradog ruled the whole of upland Glamorgan from Neath to Taff.[43] Whether the marriages had taken place before the *Four Branches* were written is perhaps not of crucial importance. It is

enough that the house of Deheubarth, like the author of the *Four Branches,* had a policy of extending the power of Dyfed (though not, of course, at the expense of Gwynedd). One way of explaining this is by attributing the *Four Branches* to a member of that house.

VIII

This concludes the arguments for Gwenllian's authorship of the *Four Branches of the Mabinogi.* It is possible, though it seems unlikely, that they can all be discounted, and *Four Branches* studies can return to the status quo taught in departments of Celtic throughout the world, in which the work is attributed to one or more unknown males, perhaps clerics or court officials, writing at some time in the eleventh or twelfth centuries. On the other hand, it is possible that Celticists as a whole will in time accept the above case for Gwenllian's authorship as proved, or at least as very probable. If so, what implications has this for future academic work?

There seem three answers here. First, the *Four Branches* will probably gain more attention, especially in North America, from students of women's writing. Princess Gwenllian may join Marie de France, St Hildegard of Bingen, Margery Kempe, and Dame Julian of Norwich in the small, privileged class of medieval women writers. If this means Celtic Studies are taken more seriously than they are at present, this must be all to the good. In the light of new evidence for authorship, students may particularly wish to examine the conclusion of Roberta Valente in her 1986 Cornell University thesis, that the *Four Branches* end in 'the total disintegration of trust between the genders'. Those accepting this view may feel that female authorship of these tales would explain such disenchantment. They may also wish to consider why the universal belief of scholars over the last century and a half has been that the *Four Branches* were written by a man.

Second, the *Four Branches* should receive increased attention from historians, not least in providing unique insights into the mentality of the Welsh ruling classes in the early twelfth century. Even so great a scholar as Sir John Lloyd failed to grasp this point, when he typified the *Mabinogion* merely as embodying 'the luxuriant and free-flowering springtime of the Welsh genius, when fancy and patriotic fervour and wistful love of the past took a hundred different shapes', etc.[44] The *Four Branches* do this, of course, but possess other elements too. Parts of them are close to being a handbook for politicians. They show native Welsh government in action: a king taking counsel, conducting diplomatic negotiations, mustering troops, invading a foreign country, and so on. Of special interest is their view of Ireland. Gruffudd ap Cynan (and thus Gwenllian) claimed descent from Brian Boru, the royal house of Leinster, and the Viking kings of Dublin. It would be gratifying to attribute aspects of the *Four Branches* to Gwenllian's Irish-Scandinavian blood. Unfortunately, the claim that Gruffudd's mother was Rhanillt, granddaughter of Sihtric Silkbeard, figures only in Gruffudd's biography, and we cannot be sure it is true.[45] No Irish source mentions it, and the *Four Branches* themselves shed no light on this point. In spite of this, the tales provide testimony of incalculable value for Welsh civilization about 1130. If their date, provenance, and authorship can be regarded as settled, they can be used by historians with more confidence than has previously been possible.[46] They should also advance the work of linguists and literary historians, especially those working on Welsh narrative prose.

Finally, the present chapter, if correct in its conclusions, should allow certain ideas about the *Four Branches* to be dropped. Some of these have been with us a long time, others are more recent. A study of early Welsh narrative, published in 1992 by Brynley Roberts, gives a good survey of them.[47] It still cites, for example, the received dating of the *Four Branches* to between 1050 and 1120. But it seems this orthodoxy, now held rigorously by nobody, may be laid to rest. All the evidence points to a date for these tales of after 1120, not before. Nor does analysis of them provide any basis for the hypotheses of their being the work of a royal clerk, or of multiple authorship.

If the *Four Branches* can be accepted with confidence as the work of Princess Gwenllian, we may close by asking what they and other sources reveal of her character. If her portrait of Rhiannon is anything to go by, she must have been a remarkable woman: resourceful, charming, generous, courageous, and noble. *Le style c'est la femme même.* Only the account by Gerald of Wales of her fatal attack on Kidwelly suggests any criticism, of a dangerous overconfidence that went with heroism. Yet, taken all in all, the image of Gwenllian from what we can guess from her life and presumed writings is an attractive one: a wife, a mother, a patriot, and surely one of the most gifted woman writers of the entire Middle Ages.

Notes

1. Owen, 40–60; Wood, 25–38; Valente, 331–45; Winward, 77–106.
2. Gruffydd, *Rhiannon*, 78–9; Mac Cana, *Branwen*, 182–90; Jackson, *International Popular Tale*, 124–30; *Branwen*, xi n. 2, xxxi n. 1.
3. Jones and Jones, 5. All references are to this translation.
4. Jarman, 131.
5. *Pwyll*, 40.
6. Pearsall, 140.
7. I owe this point to Professor John Carey of Oxford.
8. Gruffydd, *Rhiannon*, 78–9; Mac Cana, *Branwen*, 182–3; Jarman, 131.
9. Koch, 'Welsh Window', 17–52; McKenna, 'Education', 101–30; Roberts, 'Where Were the *Four Branches of the Mabinogi* Written?', 61–75.
10. Jackson, *Celtic Miscellany*, 183.
11. Echard, 196–7, 200–1.
12. Lloyd, *History*, 435, 470; *Dictionary*, 310–11; *Early Welsh Genealogical Tracts*, 47, 98, 104; *Historia*, 88; Gerald of Wales, 136–7.
13. G. V. Jones, 131–2.
14. Gruffydd, *Rhiannon*, 18.
15. Lloyd, *History*, 473; Griffiths, 100, 121; T. Llew Jones, 6–7.

16. Lloyd, *History*, 238.
17. *Branwen*, xliv.
18. *Dictionary*, 8, 61; Griffiths, 101.
19. Sims-Williams, 'Submission', 38.
20. Clarke (with an Irish Ordnance Survey map), 8.
21. *Historia*, 88.
22. Mac Cana, *Branwen*, 183–7.
23. Jackson, *International Popular Tale*, 125–8, 129–30.
24. Lloyd, *History*, 548–9; Griffiths, 106.
25. Mac Cana, *Mabinogi*, 43–4.
26. Sims-Williams, 'Submission', 61.
27. Bullock-Davies, 10–12; *Trioedd*, cxv, 287, 528.
28. Huws, '*Llyfr Gwyn Rhydderch*', 19–20, 22, and his *Llyfrau Cymraeg*, 15, 19.
29. *Oxford Book*, 28; Clancy, 130.
30. Haycock, 'Dylan Ail Ton', 26–38.
31. *Mesca Ulad*, xix-xx; *Táin*, liv.
32. *Branwen*, xxxvii-xl.
33. O'Rahilly, 68–72; Mac Eoin, 117.
34. Ó Concheanainn, 19, 30.
35. Lloyd, *History*, 260, 596–7.
36. *Pedeir Keinc*, 258–9.
37. *Gwaith Dafydd ap Gwilym*, xxxii; *Dictionary*, 839.
38. Bromwich, *Aspects*, 132–3.
39. *Culhwch*, 79–80.
40. Cf. Roberts, *Studies*, 25–40.
41. Southern, 5.
42. *Cyfranc*, xxxviii-xxxix.
43. Smith, 25–7.
44. Lloyd, 692.
45. *Early Welsh Genealogical Tracts*, 136; Flanagan, 85–6.
46. Wendy Davies, 211–12; R. R. Davies, 17–18, 69–70, 116–17.
47. Roberts, *Studies*, 96.

Politics and the *Four Branches*

If the conclusions of the previous chapter are sound, the *Four Branches* should provide material of special value for historians of Welsh politics, especially for the 1120s when (it seems) these tales were composed. If we then go on to analyse the political content of the tales, the following pattern emerges. It has five main aspects: (a) the machinery of government, especially as regards diplomacy and warfare; (b) the working of native law; (c) the policy of 'Dyfed expansionism'; (d) the constitutional status of Britain; and (e) the ethos of the tales as narratives of the reign of Henry I, when the Welsh suffered from the ascendancy of the English state.

What follows thus comments on these five aspects as revealed by a reading of the *Four Branches*. If this exercise in analysis is carried out, it will be seen the *Four Branches* reflect very well the experience of government and politics we should expect a Welsh princess of the early twelfth century to have.

I

The first branch, the tale of Pwyll, Prince of Dyfed, opens with a statement of royal status and power. 'Pwyll prince (*pendeuig*) of Dyfed was lord (*arglwyd*) over the seven cantrefs of Dyfed.'[1] Although both *pendefig* and *arglwydd* are ancient terms, since they have cognates in Old Cornish (*pendeuig, arluit*), it seems their status rose in early medieval Wales, because they are absent from the oldest poetry.[2] So there is nothing archaic in the use of these terms here. When Pwyll meets Arawn, king of Annwn, their discourse is governed by the protocol of status. Arawn refuses to greet Pwyll, though not because of his own dignity (*anryded* 'honour'), despite the fact that he would be within his rights to do so, since he is a crowned king (*brenhin corunawc*) and Pwyll a mere prince. Pwyll offers to redeem Arawn's friendship according to the dignity of Arawn. Plainly, whoever wrote this passage was sharply aware of distinctions of rank and was familiar with the Welsh law of compensation. The same familiarity with Welsh law appears in Pwyll's combat with Hafgan, where a horseman declares publicly that each is a claimant for land and territory (*tir a dayar*), reproducing a legal phrase figuring in legal texts, including the so-called Privilege of Teilo (from a tenth-century original) in the twelfth-century Book of Llandaff.[3] When Pwyll vanquishes Hafgan, he bids his followers take guidance (*kyuarwyd*) as to who his vassals may be. In this passage he claims authority using legal forms, *cyfarwydd* here being a technical expression paralleled in ninth-century Welsh.[4] From the very beginning, then, the author of the *Four Branches* shows a close knowledge of Welsh government, precedence, and law.

Other aspects of government apart from the merely legal can be found in the *Four Branches*. Even in casual phrases, the author there is revealed as one who sees the world from a position of power, and who is familiar with the responsibilities of power. Before Pwyll's encounter with Hafgan, for example, we are told that 'the tryst (*oed*) was as well remembered by the man who dwelt furthest in the whole kingdom as by himself.'[5] Whoever wrote that phrase thought naturally in terms of political dominion. Again, when Pwyll returns to Dyfed after a year's absence, he learns that his nobles (*gwyrda*) have been ruled with discernment, amity, and generosity in giving.[6] The conversation between Pwyll and his nobles (written from

If characters are noble don't you have to write to write their from p.o.v ?

the point of view of the ruler, not the ruled) suggests a writer experienced in such matters. Many other such passages could be quoted. In all of them, events are described from the point of view of somebody accustomed to rule, to be obeyed, but also to having to negotiate with individuals of high rank. The kingship depicted in the *Four Branches* demanded leadership, but also recognized the need for consultation with vassals and fellow-rulers, as we shall see. In no way was it absolute or tyrannical.

This is very evident when Pwyll and Rhiannon, after three years of marriage, are still childless. The Dyfed nobility pressurize Pwyll to divorce Rhiannon and remarry. Pwyll is closely related to them by bonds of fosterage: 'The men of the land (*gwyr y wlad*) began to feel heaviness of heart at seeing a man whom they loved as much as their lord and foster-brother without offspring.' Yet they can be formidable. They tell him frankly that he will not last for ever, and that though he may desire to remain thus, they will not suffer it from him. Pwyll asks for a year's respite, after which he will submit to their counsel. Rhiannon must, therefore, produce a child that year or be divorced. This passage thus provides remarkable evidence for the pressure that Dyfed nobles might bring on their ruler, as also for the vulnerability of a childless alien consort. Similarly, when a political crisis erupts after Rhiannon is thought to have murdered her new-born baby, the chief men (*guyrda*) of Dyfed make representation to Pwyll, requesting him to divorce his wife for this alleged crime. He compromises with them by letting her do penance instead. It is true that the political implications here have been noticed by Welsh historians from Lloyd to Pryce.[7] But the clear-eyed political understanding of decision-making here has still not been recognized for what it is. Its realism cannot be too much stressed, particularly given the traditional emphasis in *Mabinogi* studies on mythology and the supernatural.

Other political aspects of the first branch can be dealt with more briefly. The author refers casually to the fact that Teyrnon of Gwent had been Pwyll's vassal (*gwr*). So

even parts of Gwent had recognized Dyfed lordship. Even
in such a detail, we see the Dyfed patriotism which these
tales combine in so singular a way with love of Gwynedd.
When Teyrnon reaches Arberth (two miles east of Cardigan), Pwyll is said to have just arrived from making a
progress (*cylchaw*) through Dyfed.[8] How Pwyll and his
guests sat at table is described with care, again showing
the author's concern for protocol. The narrative ends
describing a greater Dyfed, of how after Pwyll's death his
son Pryderi conquered the three cantrefs of Ystrad Tywi
(Gower and east Carmarthenshire) and four cantrefs of
Ceredigion (Cardiganshire), the seven together being
called Seisyllwch, after the eighth-century ruler Seisyll.[9] It
has been pointed out that the Welsh laws, of which the
oldest surviving copy (Aberystwyth, National Library of
Wales, MS Peniarth 28, with a Latin text) dates from about
1250, make no reference to the ruler as making progresses
in person. Since we date the *Four Branches* to 1128 or thereabouts, it is probable that this practice was already obsolete by the time the author described it, although possibly
not long obsolete, since it is referred to casually and
without comment. This provides a clue as to when the
practice of *cylchaw* fell out of use (not before the later
eleventh century). As for Ystrad Tywi, we have argued
that it was there that the *Four Branches* were written, in
Cantref Mawr (between Lampeter and Llandeilo), where
Gwenllian lived after her marriage; while Seisyll was an
ancestor of her husband Gruffydd ap Rhys, who
descended from him via Angharad, wife of Rhodri Mawr
(d. 877).[10] Sir John Lloyd expressed surprise that the *Four
Branches* should allude to Seisyll. 'A very unlikely source,
to wit, the romance of Pwyll, chieftain of Dyfed, tells us
that the combined realm of Ystrad Tywi and Ceredigion
bore the name of Seisyllwg.'[11] But if, as we argue, the *Four
Branches* were written by one who had married a descendant of Seisyll, the circumstance is less surprising. Such a
detail must also create difficulties for those who associate
the production of the *Four Branches* with Clynnog Fawr,
south of Caernarfon.[12] Why should members of the Celtic

religious community there to have so scrupulously circumstantial a knowledge of the history of Dyfed? What were Dyfed political traditions to them, or their presumed audience in the Lleyn peninsula?

The first of the *Four Branches*, then, provides material showing its author's knowledge of royal government and Welsh law, as well as a familiarity with court life and claims of the Dyfed dynasty to dominion over all west Wales; while even a lord of Gwent in the far south-east is called a vassal of the prince of Dyfed.

II

The second branch, the tale of Branwen, contains more political material than the other three, including an Irish dimension which reveals much about medieval Welsh diplomacy. The opening line of the tale emphasizes the royal status of Branwen's brother, Bendigeidfran, as 'crowned king (*brenhin coronawc*) over this Island and exalted with the crown of London'.[13] His status of ruler of Gwynedd was therefore that of king (like Gwenllian's own father, Gruffudd ap Cynan), just as Pwyll's status in south-west Wales was that of prince (like Gwenllian's husband, Gruffydd ap Rhys). It is possible that Bendigeidfran's forceful and decisive character, which may be conciliatory, but can also threaten and command, owes much to memories of Gruffudd ap Cynan. It is also possible that the character of Pwyll owes something to Gruffydd ap Rhys, a lesser ruler than Gruffudd ap Cynan. If so, his unsullied chastity during his year of cohabitation with Arawn's wife would be less surprising. A woman representing her husband in fiction would not willingly represent his making love to another woman.

When King Matholwch of Ireland comes to the court at Harddlech (Harlech, Gwynedd) to seek Branwen's hand, Bendigeidfran takes counsel on the matter, since the marriage is a matter of state. Matholwch desires Branwen because he wishes to ally himself with Bendigeidfran, in order to unite Britain with Ireland and thereby strengthen them. Though we are later told Branwen is the fairest maiden in the world, this is not an official reason for the marriage. It is the calculated political reasons that are explicit. Romance has little to do with it. Whether this reflects the supposed author's experience of marriage and politics or not, it is easily related to the circumstances of her time, for Gwenllian's own marriage to Gruffydd ap Rhys had a vital political function, in helping to ally Dyfed and Gwynedd and thereby strengthen Wales against aggressors. At the wedding feast at Aberffraw in Anglesey, the seating plan is given, with Manawydan on one side of Bendigeidfran, Matholwch on the other, and Branwen next to him.[14] Protocol and precedence are again carefully observed.

However, matters turn sour following the mutilation of Matholwch's horses by Efnisien, 'the quarrelsome man we spoke of above' (for this *uchot* 'above', indicating the author's apparent visualization of an original written text, compare 'as we have described above' in the *Anglo-Saxon Chronicle* for 1090). The diplomatic crisis which Efnisien provokes is described realistically. Bendigeidfran's messengers explain that Matholwch was insulted neither with the assent of him who had authority at court (*a uedei y llys*) nor with that of any of his council (*na neb o'e kynghor*). But Matholwch is still far from mollified. Bendigeidfran appraises the situation with remarkable objectivity. He says, 'It is not to our advantage (*nyt oes ymwared*) that he go away in enmity, and we will not let him go.' Although Bendigeidfran desires good relations with the Irish, he knows he has power over them while they are in Wales, because they cannot leave against his will. He offers compensation in terms of the honour-price stipulated by Welsh law. Matholwch shall have a sound horse for each one mutilated, a silver staff as thick as his little finger and as tall as himself, and a gold plate as broad as his face. The author's familiarity with the Welsh law of honour-price (*wynebwerth*) or compensation is clear enough. Less obvious is the insight into political processes and decision-making revealed in the reaction of the Irish. They take counsel and conclude that, if they reject Bendigeidfran's terms, they are more likely to get greater shame than greater reparation. They thus accept his terms. The author's knowledge of diplomatic processes as indicated by the affair of Matholwch's horses hence indicates strong and informed political awareness. This is consistent with the attribution on other grounds of the *Four Branches* to the daughter of Gruffudd ap Cynan, a Welsh king of Irish descent with abundant experience of Irish politics.

Political events appear yet again in Matholwch's anecdote of the giant Llasar Llaes Gyfnewid. As in *Gulliver's Travels* (another fantastic-realistic masterpiece by a writer with deep experience of politics), a giant is a problem for the government. Matholwch had agreed to maintain Llasar and his wife, but they provoke a crisis when they commit outrage on his people, including *guyrda a gwragedda* 'gentles and ladies'. Matholwch's people rise, giving him a stark choice. Either the giants go or he does. He refers the problem to the council of the country. Because the giants will not go voluntarily, and cannot be ejected by force, the council devise an imaginative solution: a secret weapon, in the form of an iron chamber in which the giants can be destroyed. This works. The giants either die in the chamber, or escape and are expelled from Ireland to Wales. Even here, the author cannot help describing the action in political terms. Trapped in an iron chamber approaching white heat, the giants still 'held a council in the middle of the chamber floor' before deciding what to do.

A note here on medieval Celtic metallurgy. The iron house is heated until it is *purwen* 'white hot'. Iron reaches white heat at about 2000 degrees Fahrenheit; cast iron melts at 2192 degrees Fahrenheit (1200 degrees Celsius). However, furnaces could not produce molten iron in quantity until the thirteenth century, with the invention of bellows activated by water wheels, which allowed the iron to absorb carbon and thus liquefy. The difficulties in the twelfth century of heating iron to white heat make the

Mabinogi allusion (unique to this version of the story) quite remarkable. No wonder every smith in Ireland was needed; no wonder that the house, heaped up to roof-level with charcoal, had to be surrounded by men, each blowing a pair of bellows. White heat could not have been reached otherwise. The author, though unconcerned about swords, armour, or other militaria, did have a practical interest in processes of manufacture (as also with the accounts of saddles, shoes, and shields in the third branch). This informed awareness of twelfth-century technology is extraordinary.

It is probable that the author of the *Four Branches* used the Irish tale *Mesca Ulad* 'The Intoxication of the Ulstermen' as a source, since the Book of Leinster version of this story apparently dates from the first decades of the twelfth century, shortly before the *Four Branches* were written.[15] But three other things are also worth noting in this episode: the realism of the political processes involved in this crisis; the turbulence of opposition to the government, which seems to come from the people as a whole rather than their chief men (in contrast to the frank opinions that Pwyll received from the lords of Dyfed on Rhiannon's childlessness and supposed crime of infanticide); and the importance allocated to the royal council, acting as a formulator of policy and think tank. All three cast an interesting light on governance in Celtic society. The strength of the subject as a factor in government, and the importance of the council in decision-making, show Celtic kingship as in no way absolute. If the *Four Branches* were written by one within the royal circle, this stress on royal rule as a more problematic and vulnerable thing than might be imagined would be no surprise. Uneasy lies the head that wears a crown, etc. We may note as well that the point of view given for both Wales and Ireland is that of the ruler, to whom subject lords come, thereby creating problems. The viewpoint is not that of the ruled, who make recourse to kings in order to resolve difficulties.

A further curious parallel between history and fiction comes in Bendigeidfran's comments on these Irish giants,

'I quartered them everywhere in my domain (*kyuoeth*), and they are numerous and prosper everywhere, and fortify whatever place they happen to be in with men and arms, the best that anyone has seen.'[16] Why does the author make this curious remark? It is normally seen as a reference to the post-Roman settlements of the Irish in Lleyn, though Mac Cana remarks that 'its exact significance for eleventh-century Wales is by no means clear'.[17] Yet a reference in the life of Gruffudd ap Cynan clarifies matters here. When he conquered Gwynedd in 1075, he billeted many of his Irish or Norse-Irish followers on his new-found subjects. They soon made themselves hated. One night, fifty-two of them were murdered in their beds in Lleyn, a signal for a revolt against Gruffudd.[18] The strange allusion to Bendigeidfran's quartering of Irish warriors in his realm echoes the policy of Gruffudd ap Cynan. We may note the storyteller makes no criticism of it, though most readers might expect that giants would cause trouble in Wales as they did in Ireland. In any case, it cannot be doubted that the allusion to Irish settlements in Gwynedd has more to do with 1075 than with any memory of Irish settlements in the fifth century. It will be seen that there is complete acceptance in the *Four Branches* of that policy, no doubt because the author heard Gruffudd ap Cynan's version of it. It would, however, tend to exclude any clerical author at Clynnog Fawr in Lleyn, from whom one might expect a different view of these Irish immigrants, especially if they were billeted on monastic tenants.

The same peculiar stress on royal difficulties before popular discontent (with dislike of the Irish lords and commons) appears in the episode of Branwen's sufferings in Ireland. Matholwch rejects her and forces her to work in the kitchen, not because of his own feelings, but because of his people's 'murmuring' against her, and the taunts of his foster-brothers and men about him, all leading to an uprising (*dygyuor*) which threatened to depose him.[19] In this Matholwch provides a striking contrast with Pwyll. Pressure concerning their wives is put on both Pwyll and Matholwch by their subjects. But Pwyll is better at handling the situation than is Matholwch. Matholwch agrees to put away Branwen, Pwyll refuses to put away Rhiannon, though even Pwyll has to compromise on the matter of penance.

Matholwch's weak leadership contrasts sharply with the conspicuous resolution of Bendigeidfran on hearing of his sister's humiliation. This whole passage is of great interest, in showing twelfth-century Welsh government in action. Here it is natural to associate Bendigeidfran's decisiveness with the figure of Gruffudd ap Cynan, a king notable for dynamic action, including (in 1081) a successful invasion of Wales from Ireland.[20] (Though critics like Morfydd Owen stress Branwen's vulnerability and powerlessness, a princess who can summon an army and navy to her rescue is hardly as vulnerable and powerless as other women.) When Bendigeidfran hears of Branwen's distress, he at once sends messengers from Caernarfon to muster all Britain. When the levy of the 154 districts arrives, he addresses them, complaining of the affliction on his sister. They then take counsel. They decide to invade Ireland, leaving seven men as overlords (*tywyssogyon*) over Britain, these men acting as stewards (*kynueissait*), with Bran's son Cradawg as their chief steward.

Two points may be made here. First, Ifor Williams suggested that the 154 districts of Britain correspond to the 156 cantrefs and commots of Wales as recorded from an early source in Aberystwyth, National Library of Wales, MS Peniarth 163, written in 1543 by Gruffydd Hiraethog, bard and herald. The author of the *Four Branches* was certainly familiar with the district (*gwlad*), cantref, and commot (*cymwt*) as Welsh administrative regions.[21] These units apparently took their final form in about 1100.[22] So we may infer that the writer, who alludes to the commots of Anglesey, the cantrefs of Dyfed, the commot of Mochnant in Powys, and so on, had a good knowledge of Welsh administration, and conjectured that Celtic Britain had been divided into just the same number of units for mustering troops. The author's knowledge of the administrative machinery by which war was waged in medieval Wales, and the steps taken to ensure proper government in the absence of the ruler, is exact and factual. Yet again, this implies an author close to the centre of government.

Second, it will be noted that Bendigeidfran in Gwynedd seems to have greater forces at his disposal, and to suffer less opposition from nobles, than Pwyll does in Dyfed. This may reflect more than merely the difference between the King of the Island of the Mighty (Britain) and the prince of Dyfed. The nobility of Dyfed were notably less docile than the nobility of Gwynedd. A. H. Williams described the *gwyrda* of Deheubarth or southern Wales as challengers of royal authority, 'tenacious' of their rights, and 'often ready' to declare that the king had acted wrongly or oppressively.[23] In the light of Williams's analysis (which was written without reference to the *Four Branches*), we understand better why Pwyll's subjects could summon him to an assembly at Preseli in the hills of Dyfed, and speak to him so boldly, declaring 'Thou wilt not last for ever, and though thou desire to remain thus, we will not suffer it from thee.' If the authorship for the *Four Branches* proposed here is correct, the author would be well situated to contrast the political climate of Gwynedd with the more turbulent one of West Wales. Hence the differing powers and need for accommodation of Pwyll and Bendigeidfran, who in varying ways correspond to Gruffydd ap Rhys and Gruffudd ap Cynan.

Bendigeidfran and his army overcome anti-invasion devices planted by the Irish (magnets at the bottom of the Liffey, which suck ships down). The Irish then sue for peace. The account of the negotiations makes fascinating reading. They reveal certain perennial perceptions of Ireland. With a British army on Irish soil, the author implies that the Irish must admit defeat. Messengers come to Bendigeidfran with Matholwch's greetings, 'showing how through his good will nothing but good should come his way'. Matholwch is to give the kingship of Ireland to Branwen's son, Gwern, who is to be invested in Bendigeidfran's presence. (The word used is *ystynnu* 'extend, reach out', used in Welsh law in the sense 'present, confer'.) Bendigeidfran, knowing he is in a position of strength, demands better terms. Matholwch's council then tell him to build Bendigeidfran a house, place his kingship in Bendigeidfran's gift, and do him homage (*gwra idaw*). After taking council like a constitutional monarch, Bendigeidfran accepts these terms. The author takes care to inform us of a woman's crucial role in these negotiations. 'And that was all done by counsel of Branwen, and lest the land be laid waste she did that.'[24] This significant expression shows the constant concern in the *Four Branches* for good government (now recognized by many critics), as also (more singularly) the influence of women on events.

All seems set fair. But everything is ruined by treachery. Ireland and Britain are both devastated by war. In Bendigeidfran's absence, Caswallon son of Beli conquers the Island of the Mighty and is crowned king in London. Conscious of the loss of Britain, the author of the *Four Branches* portrays Caswallon as a usurper, wresting authority from its rightful possessors, just as he is also an enemy with a dishonourable secret weapon (a mantle of invisibility) against whom resistence is futile. In this Caswallon plays much the role of Henry I (1100–1135), who through military might exerted strict control over Wales. Had the *Four Branches* been written after 1135 in the time of the Anarchy (which the Welsh fully exploited), they would hardly have represented the political authority of London as so remorseless.[25] Even after 1154, when Henry II made vigorous attempts to undo what the Welsh had regained, he eventually had to come to terms. In their pessimistic attitude to Wales's relationship with government in London, the *Four Branches* can thus be related to the political climate of between 1116, when Gruffydd ap Rhys's insurrection ended in failure, and 1136, when the Welsh rose again against Norman power.

Even more than the first branch, therefore, the second of the *Four Branches* reveals an author possessed of political information, experience, and insight deriving from the highest levels, all described with natural confidence and conviction. The verisimilitude gained thereby ensures the success of the narrative. This familiarity with or inside knowledge of politics strongly indicates that the author was a member of the Welsh governing class.

III

When we move on to the third of the *Four Branches*, the tale of Manawydan, we find far less political material than in the others. Nevertheless, it reminds us that life goes on even after catastrophe. Pryderi gives good advice to Manawydan, who is grieving for the death of his brother Bendigeidfran and the usurpation of the crown of London by Caswallon. Pryderi proposes the partition of his territories, with the seven cantrefs of Dyfed to be allotted to Manawydan and the seven of Seisyllwg to remain in Pryderi's hands. This decision merits attention. It is part of the extraordinary consideration given to Gwynedd (and no other part of Wales) throughout the tales that a Gwynedd prince should actually be granted the ancient realm of Dyfed. One says 'extraordinary'; though it would of course be far less so if the author were from Gwynedd and living in Dyfed. That would explain the remarkable consideration here given to the dignity of the royal house of Gwynedd, otherwise all but inexplicable. (It also explains the consideration shown in the fourth branch for a Dyfed army defeated by Gwynedd forces, as noted below.) Pryderi goes to Oxford to render homage to Caswallon (who thereby parallels Henry I in his last years, as argued above).

IV

Full political activity returns in the fourth branch. This provides detailed information both on the workings of government in Gwynedd, and on its relationships with

Dyfed. It begins with a constitutional statement. Math was lord (*arglwydd*) over Gwynedd, and Pryderi lord over twenty-one cantrefs in the South. These were the seven of Dyfed, the seven of Seisyllwg, and the seven of Morgannwg or Glamorgan.[26] The vision of a greater Dyfed develops the theme of Dyfed expansionism that the author is careful to mention at the end of the first branch. We may also note that *arglwydd* is accurately used for Math's status. After Bendigeidfran's death and Caswallon's usurpation of the crown of London, the ruler of Gwynedd is no longer a king (*brenin*). Since *arglwydd* is known to alternate with *brenin* in the law books, the new status of Gwynedd's lord is shown by use of another word.[27] The author of the *Four Branches* may be vague on many matters: but not royal rank.

The third branch had been one of scenes of pastoral tranquillity, celebrating the beauty of Dyfed and its abundance in game, honey, and fish. But the fourth branch returns to the theme of war. In order that Gilfaethwy may gain Goewin, his lord's handmaid, Gwydion starts a war between Gwynedd and Dyfed. He goes to seek magic swine from Pryderi in Ceredigion, which Pryderi says he cannot give, because there is a covenant (*ammot*) between him and his country.[28] The text again shows familiarity with Welsh law, where *amod* is the ordinary word for 'contract'.[29]

Gwydion devises a way to release Pryderi from his bond. Pryderi takes counsel and accepts Gwydion's offer, but soon finds he has been deceived. War follows. The hosts of Gwynedd and Dyfed clash in the middle of the districts of Maenawr Bennardd and Maenawr Coed Alun. ('Pennarth' is still the name of a farm between Clynnog and Llanllyfni, some seven miles south of Caernarfon; 'Coed Alun' is a mansion facing Caernarfon Castle across the river Saint.) The men of Dyfed retreat south to Nant Call, near the modern hamlet of Pant Glas, on the main road eleven miles south of Caernarfon. Slaughter continues. Then they retreat to Dolbenmaen, four miles southeast, still on the main road south. There they make a truce, giving twenty-four hostages of noble rank (*gwyrda*).

The curiously circumstantial account of fighting on the strategic route south of Caernarfon still followed by the A487, through the pass between the mountains of Snowdonia and those of Lleyn, is worth emphasis. Although fighting often occurs in the *Four Branches*, the author elsewhere shows no interest in describing it in detail. We lack the loving descriptions of swords or spears or the extended accounts of combat in Homer or *Beowulf* or Malory.[30] Why this exception? The reason is surely a family one. In the rising of 1075, Gwenllian's father had lost a battle against insurgents from Gwynedd who were backed by troops from Powys. Gruffudd was defeated at Bron yr Erw, in the upland gap two miles wide by Nant Call, perhaps near Brysgyni, east of Clynnog Fawr on the coast.[31] Nothing would be easier for the presumed author of the *Four Branches* than to set this campaign in the region her own father had fought in. This gives a more compelling explanation for the campaign's location than the belief of Professor Sims-Williams and Dr Brynley Roberts that it was because the tales are the work of the religious of Clynnog: for which there is no evidence in the text.

The war ends when Gwydion kills Pryderi in single combat. The delicacy with which the author comments on the defeat of Dyfed is worth stressing. 'The men of the South set forth with bitter lamentation towards their own land. Nor was it strange. They had lost their lord, and many of their noblemen, and their horses, and their arms for the most part.' Similarly, the author is careful to mention how, at Gwydion's request, Math in his triumph agrees to free the hostages from Dyfed. Why should our author care for the feelings of the defeated? This is not a common trait in literature, except perhaps in the greatest writers (as in the words of Vergil on Cleopatra after Actium, who hears the Nile sorrowfully calling the defeated to the shelter of his waters). But we need not seek such extraordinary humanity in the *Mabinogi* author, who (despite Branwen's reflection that two good islands have been destroyed because of her) does not waste overmuch compassion on the treacherous Irish. The unusual consideration here for the men of Dyfed is sufficiently accounted for by the hypothesis of a Gwynedd writer working at the court of Dyfed. No other account of the *Mabinogi*, it would seem, answers this question so cogently.

Some unexpected points emerge in the description of Gwynedd in the aftermath of war. Math marries Goewin, making the quite remarkable statement that he will give the authority (*medyant*) over his realm into her hands.[32] This deserves comment. It is usually considered on the basis of the laws that Welsh queens had no political power, despite servants, privileges, and a third of the king's income from his personal land.[33] Math's declaration is thus a striking one, since Ifor Williams noted that Middle Welsh *medyant* means 'authority', not 'possession' (unlike modern *meddiant*).[34] It is hard to recall from elsewhere in medieval literature a similar acknowledgement of female political authority. Another political feature comes out in Math's treatment of Gwydion and Gilfaethwy. They are making a circuit of the land, but return to Math's control when 'a ban (*guahard*) on their meat and drink went out against them'. Evidently a lord had the right to withdraw the render of a circuit from kinsfolk benefiting from it.[35]

The remaining political aspects of the last branch can be dealt with briefly. When Lleu enters the narrative and marries Blodeuedd, he is given the cantref of Dinoding as his domain, since (as Gwydion points out), 'It is not easy for a man without territory (*heb gyfoeth*) to maintain himself (*gossymdeithaw*).' The author tells us Dinoding is the region now represented by the Gwynedd commotes of Eifionydd (around Cricieth) and Ardudwy (from the Vale of Ffestiniog to Barmouth). Lleu sets up his court as Mur Castell, the old Roman fort of Tomen y Mur, on an exposed hilltop 1000 feet up near Trawsfynydd. All are content with his rule.[36]

This episode again reveals the priorities of a ruling class, for whom the provision of a domain for a young lord is a matter of importance. (The author of the *Four Branches* shows almost as practical and realistic an attitude to the need for an income as Jane Austen does.) But Lleu's happiness ends tragically when his wife has an affair with Gronw, lord of the commot of Penllyn immediately east of Ardudwy, around Bala. Gronw stabs Lleu (who, transformed into an eagle, flies away) and seizes Ardudwy. Yet Lleu is eventually discovered, given his normal form, and restored to health at Caer Dathyl (perhaps the 'Toot Hill' at Caernarfon) with the aid of the best doctors of Gwynedd. From his stronghold of Penllyn, Gronw sends envoys to ask if Lleu will accept land or territory (compare the legal expression *tir a dayar* above) or gold or silver for his injury (*sarhaet* 'insult, act of injury or wrong', another legal term).[37] He will not. Lleu eventually slays Gronw, regains his lands, and rules them prosperously, eventually becoming lord of Gwynedd. Here the tale ends.

V

What basis does the above provide for future research on the *Four Branches*, especially in the University of Wales? The present analysis of their politics is far from exhaustive. It has hardly touched upon such issues (important for the Welsh governing class) as fosterage, honour and shame, or the etiquettes of hunting or feasting, with their special protocols. There is also room for a monograph on the legal vocabulary and thinking of the *Four Branches* in the light of recent work on Welsh law, particularly as regards differences in legal practice between the various parts of Wales.

However, the five aspects outlined at the beginning of this chapter come out clearly enough. The author had an intimate knowledge of Welsh government; an easy familiarity with Welsh law; a lyrical love of Dyfed, and pride in its expansion (which went with a respect for Gwynedd and its military power); a belief in the older British constitution, in which the island of Britain is a political unity under one Celtic king (a theory leaving no room for invaders); and an awareness that that unity, symbolized by the crown of London, has been usurped by force, which must be acknowledged, resistence to it being pointless.

These attitudes, together with all other aspects of the narratives (especially as regards topography and gender), accord perfectly with what we should expect of a Gwynedd princess of high intelligence and unique artistic gifts, who was married to a Dyfed prince, and who came to maturity during the reign of Henry I. The more the *Four Branches* are examined in detail, the more such analysis confirms the contention of the present writer that these tales are the work of Gwenllian (*c*.1097–1136), daughter of King Gruffudd ap Cynan of Gwynedd.

Yet is this hypothesis subject to falsifiability, in the way Sir Karl Popper approached scientific and social ideas? Are there techniques by which the view that Gwenllian composed the *Four Branches* could be disproved? With so much evidence provided by the text, this must surely be so. There seem to be two headings. First are symptoms of the text which one could not attribute to a Welsh princess. If, for example, it could be proved that the author of the *Four Branches* had a professional training in Welsh bardic poetry, the attribution to Gwenllian would have to be rejected, since training as a bard was in the early Middle Ages restricted to men. If those who maintain the *Four Branches* are the work of a court poet can produce such evidence, then Gwenllian's authorship will, of course, have to be rejected. Alternatively, if it could be shown that the author had a knowledge of Biblical or patristic learning or of canon law, then we should know Gwenllian could not have composed these tales, since a medieval princess would hardly have such ecclesiastical knowledge. Or again, if it could be demonstrated that the author had a familiarity with Irish tradition and culture explicable only by long residence in Ireland, they could hardly be the work of Gwenllian, who may have visited Ireland in 1127, but who is not known to have lived there for an extended period.

Second, Gwenllian's authorship could be ruled out on the grounds of date. If any reference could be found proving the *Four Branches* must have been written before about 1120, when Gwenllian had reached her majority, or after 1136, when she was executed, then her authorship would be out of the question. If, for example, it could be shown that the *Four Branches* are influenced by Geoffrey of Monmouth's *History of the Kings of Britain*, then they could not be the work of Gwenllian, since Geoffrey published his history shortly after her death in January 1136 and not before it.

If, however, the attribution of the *Four Branches* to Gwenllian can be accepted, then further research on them will deepen our understanding of the period when they were written, whether they deal with the vocabulary, narrative techniques, learning, textual transmission, representation of material culture, or social or political outlook of the tales. The *Four Branches of the Mabinogi* hence offer a wealth of material to historians and others. Providing a remarkable window on twelfth-century Wales and Ireland, they are amongst the glories of Wales, the work of a woman writer who was a princess of the royal houses of Gwynedd and Dyfed.

Notes

1. Lloyd, *History*, map facing 816; Jones and Jones, 3; Rees, plate 28; *Dictionary*, xxi; *Pwyll*, 1.
2. Binchy, 23; Wendy Davies, *Patterns*, 14.
3. *Pwyll*, 4–5, 28; Wendy Davies, *Patterns*, 82–3.
4. *Pedeir Keinc*, 111; Jenkins and Owen, 53–4.
5. Jones and Jones, 6; *Pwyll*, 4.
6. Jones and Jones, 8; *Pwyll*, 7.
7. Lloyd, *History*, 291 n. 36; Pryce, 92–3.
8. Jones and Jones, 21, 22, 24; *Pwyll*, 21, 22, 23.
9. *Pedeir Keinc*, 156; *Pwyll*, 40–1.
10. *Early Welsh Genealogical Tracts*, 49.
11. Lloyd, *Story*, 12.
12. Sims-Williams, 'Clas Beuno', 111–27; Roberts, 'Where Were the *Four Branches of the Mabinogi* Written?', 61–75.

13. Jones and Jones, 25; *Branwen*, 1.
14. Jones and Jones, 26; *Branwen*, 2.
15. Mac Cana, *Branwen*, 16–23.
16. Jones and Jones, 31; *Branwen*, 7.
17. *Pedeir Keinc*, 185; Mac Cana, *Branwen*, 6 n. 1; *Branwen*, 29.
18. Lloyd, *History*, 382; *Dictionary*, 310; *Historia*, 10.
19. Jones and Jones, 32; *Branwen*, 8.
20. *Dictionary*, 310.
21. *Pedeir Keinc*, 191; *Branwen*, 27.
22. Wendy Davies, *Wales*, 235–6.
23. A. H. Williams, 140.
24. Jones and Jones, 34–5; *Branwen*, 11–12.
25. Walker, 45–7.
26. *Pedeir Keinc*, 67; Jones and Jones, 55.
27. *Welsh Law*, 191.
28. *Pedeir Keinc*, 69; Jones and Jones, 57.
29. *Welsh Law*, 190.
30. Cf. Sisam, 12–13.
31. Lloyd, *History*, 383; *Historia*, 68–9.
32. *Pedeir Keinc*, 74; Jones and Jones, 61.
33. A. H. Williams, 144.
34. *Pedeir Keinc*, 228; Jones and Jones, 61.
35. *Pedeir Keinc*, 74; Jones and Jones, 61.
36. *Pedeir Keinc*, 84; Jones and Jones, 68.
37. *Pedeir Keinc*, 91; Jones and Jones, 74.

The *Four Branches* and Hywel ab Owain Gwynedd

The previous chapter suggested further research would confirm the present thesis. This chapter does just that, with a linguistic test on the *Four Branches*. Amongst Gwenllian's nephews was Hywel (d. 1170), an illegitimate son of her brother Owain Gwynedd. Hywel, who became lord of southern Ceredigion in 1139, had a military career, and was eventually killed in battle against his half-brothers soon after his father's death.[1] He was also a gifted poet, eight of whose poems have survived. If Gwenllian composed the *Four Branches*, we might expect parallels between them and the writings of her nephew, especially in vocabulary. They would reflect the usages of the Gwynedd royal family in the early twelfth century. Whether this is so or not should emerge as we go through the texts in detail.

Before we do this, however, one point should be made clear. When we refer to an author 'writing' the *Four Branches*, by 'writing' is meant 'putting into or producing in literary form, bringing out (a book or literary work) as author', as defined by the *Oxford English Dictionary*. This writer has never stated (though some Welsh critics think he has) that the hand which wrote down the *Four Branches* belonged to their author. (It is likely that, if Gwenllian did compose the *Four Branches*, she was illiterate.) This paper says no more on the composition of the *Four Branches*, their relation to their sources, and what might be called their 'prehistory'; but readers who wish to know more are referred to the writings of Professor Sioned Davies, who has worked on this difficult question for many years.[2]

I

When we go through the *Four Branches* and Hywel's poems, we find many correspondences of vocabulary, such as *duüno* 'agree', *gosteg* 'silence', or *taeru* 'maintain'. Yet these may be left aside. The only words useful for our purposes are rare ones, including poetic words seldom used in prose, and vice versa. Of these there are at least eleven: *brawdfaeth* 'foster brother', *canwelw* 'pale white', *dihenydd* 'execution', *gorawenus* 'joyous', *gweilgi* 'the sea', *hyweddu* 'to tame', *maranedd* 'treasure', *pali* 'brocaded silk', *pall* 'tent', *parabl* 'utterance', and *peddestrig* 'walking; a walking'. We may also add the prefix *mab-* 'appertaining to a child'. Does scrutiny of these words suggest a special relationship between the *Four Branches* and Hywel's poems?

1. *brawdfaeth*
Brawdfaeth 'foster brother' (sometimes written *brawd maeth*) is not common in early Welsh. The earliest recorded prose instance is in the story of Pwyll, where the men of Dyfed grieve to see him 'their lord and foster-brother (*brawduaeth*)' without children.[3] The word is rarer in poetry than prose. Lloyd-Jones cites three instances only.[4] Of these, one is from Hywel ab Owain Gwynedd, who in a love-poem regrets that Gwerfyl ignores him: 'The king's brother's wife (*gwraig brawduaeth brenhin*) denies me.'[5] Of the other instances, one is from Cynddelw, the other from an elegy on Hywel by Peryf ap Cedifor, who laments his four brothers that 'fell near their foster-brother (*brawd uaeth*)', who was Hywel himself.[6]

Fosterage is as important in the *Four Branches* as it was in the life of twelfth-century Gwynedd. Pwyll has foster-brothers; Pryderi is fostered by Pendaran Dyfed; Branwen's son Gwern is fostered 'in the very best place in

Ireland'; Teyrnon's wife expected her foster-son Pryderi to support her in later life.[7] In the tale of Math, Gronw Bebyr's warband and foster-brothers refuse to take a fatal blow in his stead, which was a shameful act.[8]

Conclusion: the prose word *brawdfaeth* is recorded in poetry three times only, once in a poem by Hywel ab Owain, elsewhere in an elegy on him. It thus seems a significant link between the *Four Branches* and Hywel's work.

— ⋅•⋅ —

2. *canwelw*

Canwelw 'pale, whitish'. This word is uncommon. Dictionaries cite six examples only from literary texts, including one from *Canu Aneirin* (line 1470), two from *The Dream of Rhonabwy*, and one from the *Four Branches*, of the pale white horse which Rhiannon rides on past the mound at Arberth, near Cardigan. Lloyd-Jones quotes one instance of *canwelw* from the poets of the princes, from Cynddelw. But Hywel talks of returning from exile on a *welw gann* 'white steed'.[9]

Conclusion: the rare word *canwelw* is used once in the *Four Branches*, once by the poets of the princes; but Hywel uses the variant *welw gann*. A significant connection is thus possible.

— ⋅•⋅ —

3. *dihenydd*

Dihenydd 'execution' is common in prose (the Laws, Book of the Anchorite, *Peredur*) but rare in the poets of the princes. Lloyd-Jones cites four instances from the latter, one from Hywel, the others of the fourteenth century.[10] The word is familiar in the *Four Branches*. In the tale of Pwyll, Gwawl son of Clud protests that being trampled in a bag is no fit death (*dihenyd*) for him; Manawydan prepares to execute the doom (*dihenyd*) of hanging on a mouse. We might add that the verbal form is used by Rhiannon's women, who know being put to death (*dieny-*

dyaw) would be small vengeance for her son's loss, and Manawydan and Pryderi, who hear their enemies want to kill them (*dienydyaw*).[11] Hywel uses the noun in a poem in praise of Gwynedd, where he declares 'God be mindful of me when dying (*uy nihenyt*).[12]

Conclusion: *dihenydd* is a familiar form in prose, including the *Four Branches*, but rare in verse. The one early poet of the princes to use it is Hywel. It suggests, therefore, a significant link.

— ·•· —

4. *gorawenus*
Gorawenus 'joyful, exultant' is another prose word. In the *Four Branches* it occurs once, in the tale of Math, describing the return 'in joy and exultation (*gorawenus*)' of the men of Gwynedd after victory over the men of Dyfed (whose defeat and release of whose prisoners is described with unusual consideration).[13] It also occurs in a collection of the Blessed Virgin's miracles, the life of Gruffudd ap Cynan, tales of the Seven Sages of Rome, and so on. In poetry Lloyd-Jones records it only twice, from Llygad Gwr (of *c*.1268), and from Hywel's praise of a girl in summer, when men are 'high-hearted (*gorawenus*) before a brave lord'.[14]

Conclusion: *gorawenus* is a prose word, used once in the *Four Branches*. Of two recorded instances in the poets of the princes, one is in the work of Hywel ab Owain. It therefore provides a significant parallel.

— ·•· —

5. *gweilgi*
Gweilgi 'sea, ocean' is a somewhat poetic word, though Lloyd-Jones also cites it from prose, especially Welsh translations of Geoffrey of Monmouth. In Hywel it refers to a castle, 'Gleaming bright it rises beside the sea (*gweilgi*)'.[15] In the *Four Branches* it occurs three times, all in the tale of Branwen, all referring to the Irish Sea.[16] It seems not to occur elsewhere in the *Mabinogion*.

Conclusion: a link here is possible, although *gweilgi* occurs too often in the Welsh *Brut* to be taken as a mainly poetic word.

— ·•· —

6. *hywedd*
Hywedd 'tamed, docile, broken in (of a horse)' is important in the present test. The University of Wales Dictionary quotes it twice from medieval prose, from the Welsh laws, and from the tale of Pwyll. Teyrnon's wife advises her husband to have a colt broken in (*hywedu*, a unique recorded instance of the verb in medieval prose). When he agrees, she bids the grooms have the horse broken in (*uot yn hywed*) for her foster-son Gwri.[17] Of six instances in verse, one is from Hywel, who says of Gwynedd, 'I love its soldiers and its trained steeds (*meirch hywet*).'[18]

Conclusion: *hywedd* is a word rare in medieval prose, but familiar in medieval poetry. Its use in both Hywel and the *Four Branches* is thus a significant parallel.

— ·•· —

7. *maranedd*
Maranedd 'treasure' is another important form. It is a poetic word, effectively restricted to the poets of the princes. Hywel applies it to Gwynedd, saying he loves 'its wide wilderness and its wealth (*maranedd*).'[19] The sole recorded instance of the word in prose is in the tale of Pwyll, who comes to the court of Rhiannon's father, where all its resources (*holl uaranned*) are placed at his direction.[20]

Conclusion: the unique prose use of this poetic word in the *Four Branches* is striking and distinctive.

— ·•· —

8 *pali*
Pali 'brocaded silk' (Old French *palie*) is well known as a foreign borrowing in the *Four Branches*. It is familiar in medieval prose but extremely rare in the poets of the

princes. The University of Wales Dictionary records one
instance, from the deathbed poem of the Gwynedd bard
Meilyr (fl. *c*.1100–37), who wrote Gruffudd ap Cynan's
elegy.[21] But another occurs in Hywel's line 'None wins a
mantle who looks not at silk (*pali*)'.[22] *Pali* occurs three
times in the tale of Pwyll, once in that of Branwen, as well
as in the later *Mabinogion* tales of Peredur, Gereint, and
Rhonabwy's Dream.[23]

Conclusion: *pali* is a prose word familiar from the *Four
Branches*. It is recorded twice in early medieval poetry, in
the work of Hywel and Meilyr Brydydd. It is therefore
especially significant in this context.

— .◦. —

9 *pall*

Pall 'tent' is another borrowing, almost certainly from
French *pa(i)lle* 'cloth of silk; covering, tent'. The University
of Wales Dictionary records five instances of it before
1300: two from the bard Cynddelw, one from Hywel, two
from the *Four Branches*.[24] Hywel praises Gwenlliant, 'she
from the tent'.[25] In the story of Branwen, we hear how at
her marriage in Aberffraw the courts of Britain and
Ireland were feasted in tents (*palleu*), as also at their later
reconciliation.[26]

Conclusion: the use of this uncommon word by both
Hywel and the author of the *Four Branches* is an important
linguistic parallel.

— .◦. —

10. *parabl* 'utterance'

This is yet another borrowing, from Old French *parab(o)le*
(a Middle English loan can be ruled out here). It occurs in
prose in the *Four Branches*, *Peredur*, the *Brut*, and the Welsh
version of *Bevis of Hampton*.[27] In the *Four Branches* it comes
in the tale of Pwyll, in the pillow talk of Arawn and his
wife, when he spoke to her (*a farabyl a dywot ef*) three times
before she answered.[28] In verse it occurs in Cynddelw's
death-bed poem and a love-poem by Hywel, where he

says of the girl that no 'unseemly speech (*parabl*) will come from her lips'.[29]

Conclusion: the use of this third loan from French is a further significant link between Hywel's poetry and the *Four Branches*.

— .◦. —

11. *peddestrig*
Peddestrig 'walking; a walking' is an unusual word, more common in Welsh prose than in verse. In prose it occurs in the *Four Branches*, *Gereint*, *Peredur*, an account of St Edmund of Abingdon's miracles; in verse, in Hywel ab Owain, and Cynddelw.[30] In the *Four Branches* it is used in the tale of Pwyll of the servant following Rhiannon, and in the tale of Manawydan of a limping mouse.[31] Hywel uses it to address a girl in a love-poem, where he asks 'Pacing (*peddestrig*), pleading, shall I have a tryst?'[32]

Conclusion: the appearance of this curious expression provides some evidence for a link here.

— .◦. —

12. Finally, Hywel has a unique fondness for the prefix *mab-* 'relating to a child'. He uses the words *mabddysg* 'what is learnt as a child' (also used by Llywarch ap Llywelyn, twice), the very rare *mabinaidd* 'child-like', and *mabwraig* 'young girl' (twice).[33] There is nothing like this anywhere else in Welsh poetry.

Conclusion: Hywel's linking of words beginning *mab-* is a singular trick of his style. It may perhaps point to a link with the rare word *mabinogi* of the *Four Branches of the Mabinogi*.

II

What then, does the above suggest? It seems there is an extremely close relation between the language of the *Four Branches* and that of Hywel ab Owain. This is the more striking given the fewness of Hywel's poems. We have only eight of them, covering just over six pages of text in the diplomatic edition. To find so many coincidences of vocabulary between the *Four Branches* and so small a poetic corpus surely indicates that poet and storyteller had an all but identical linguistic background. But this conclusion may be false. If so, critics should be able to point to important differences in vocabulary (to say nothing of syntax and grammar) between the *Four Branches* and Hywel's poetry, which would effectively disprove the writer's view that they are work of aunt and nephew. One would certainly wish to see evidence of this in print.

If, however, nothing of the kind can be found, we can accept that the author of the *Four Branches* had linguistic contacts not only with Gwynedd, but with the Gwynedd royal family. The refined, lucid Welsh used by that author would be the language of the Gwynedd court. There is, of course, nothing remarkable in this conclusion. Professor Sioned Davies has suggested in her major study that the *Four Branches* are the work of a Gwynedd court official, and nothing in the actual language of Hywel ab Owain and the *Four Branches* goes against this. What is difficult, however, is to reconcile her hypothesis with non-linguistic aspects of the stories, such as their love of Dyfed, with knowledge of Dyfed geography, and support for Dyfed's political expansion (eastwards, one notes, not northwards).

The writer therefore submits that there is one person whose circumstances accord with the distinctive linguistic, historical, geographical, social, and political profile of the *Four Branches*, and that is Gwenllian, daughter of Gruffudd ap Cynan.

If this conclusion is correct, its main importance is for Welsh studies. But we may note it has implications for Irish studies as well. They seem twofold. Gwenllian reached her majority before about 1120 and died in January 1136. This allows us to date the *Four Branches* to 1120-1136, with a likely dating of 1128 or somewhat later, when Gwenllian had gained experience of life and when her husband (and herself?) had been exiled in Ireland (presumably in Dublin) in 1127, which would help explain the Irish elements in the *Four Branches*.

If so, a date of about 1128 for the *Four Branches* offers Irish scholars two things. First, it provides a picture of Irish society as seen by an outsider in 1127 or thereabouts. This was a period of turmoil, especially in Leinster, whose king had died in 1126, leaving a power vacuum. In 1127 the Norse of Dublin had submitted to Toirrdelbach Ua Conchobair (d. 1156) of Connacht, who had arrived in force, and who appointed his son Conchobar (d. 1144) as their ruler.[34] The confused state of Ireland in this period, particularly Leinster, may lie behind the complex picture of unrest there presented in the tale of Branwen. This exists at levels from male domestic violence against Branwen to civil unrest and full-scale military confrontation.

Secondly, if the *Four Branches* were written in 1128 or soon after, this gives a cut-off point for the dating of Irish narratives used in it, especially *Mesca Ulad*. The implications of this need not be gone into here, but they may be useful to Irish scholars, to whom precisely-dated Welsh texts would provide a foothold in what Kathleen Mulchrone described unflatteringly as the *portach* of Middle Irish, a linguistic morass, in which the researcher may disappear without trace.[35]

Notes

1. *Dictionary*, 404–5.
2. Sioned Davies, *Crefft y Cyfarwydd*.
3. Jones and Jones, 17; *Geiriadur*, 312; *Pwyll*, 17, and cf. 37 n.
4. Lloyd-Jones, 73.
5. *Oxford Book*, 26; Clancy, 133; and cf. *Gwaith Llywelyn Fardd I*.

6. *Oxford Book*, 29; Clancy, 135.

7. *Pwyll*, 37 n.

8. *Pedeir Keinc*, 92; Jones and Jones, 74.

9. Lloyd-Jones, 107; *Geiriadur*, 419; Clancy, 132; *Trioedd*, 104.

10. *Geirfa*, 350; cf. *Gwaith Bleddyn Ddu*, 30.

11. *Pedeir Keinc*, 17, 20, 53, 62; Jones and Jones, 16, 18, 44, 51; *Pwyll*, 15, 17.

12. *Llawysgrif*, 316; Clancy, 132.

13. *Pedeir Keinc*, 73; Jones and Jones, 60.

14. *Oxford Book*, 28; Clancy, 129.

15. *Llawysgrif*, 320; Clancy, 130.

16. Jones and Jones, 25, 33; *Branwen*, 1, 9.

17. Jones and Jones, 21; *Pwyll*, 20.

18. *Llawysgrif*, 316; Clancy, 132.

19. *Oxford Book*, 26; Clancy 132.

20. Jones and Jones, 12; *Pwyll*, 12.

21. *Oxford Book*, 23; Clancy, 117.

22. *Llawysgrif*, 320; Clancy, 130.

23. *Geiriadur*, 2674; *Pwyll*, 65; *Branwen*, 67.

24. *Geiriadur*, 2676.

25. *Llawysgrif*, 317; cf. Clancy, 133.

26. Jones and Jones, 26, 29; *Branwen*, 3, 5.

27. *Geiriadur*, 2684.

28. Jones and Jones, 8; *Pwyll*, 6.

29. *Oxford Book*, 28; Clancy, 130.

30. *Geiriadur*, 2713.

31. *Pedeir Keinc*, 9, 10, 60; Jones and Jones, 9, 10, 50; *Pwyll*, 8, 9.

32. *Oxford Book*, 28; Clancy, 130.

33. *Geiriadur*, 2294, 2295, 2296.

34. Ó Corráin, 154; Byrne, 270, 301.

35. Mac Eoin, 109–37; Mac Gearailt, 'Language', 167–216.

Welsh Tradition and the
Baker's Daughter in *Hamlet*

Ophelia's enigmatic remark in *Hamlet*, 'They say the owl
was a baker's daughter' (IV.v.42–3), has unexpected
analogues. Jenkins here referred to a modern folktale
(noted in Douce's *Illustrations of Shakespear* of 1807) on a
baker's daughter who stinted Christ when he sought
bread, and was thus turned into an owl.[1] The tale is known
from Britain and North America only, though stories of a
man (not a woman) punished by transformation into an
owl are old and widespread.[2] Jenkins also noted that the
owl's mournful cry has been regarded as lamenting the
death of love (like Ophelia's songs); that a modern Welsh
superstition takes the owl's cry as marking the loss of
virginity; and that bakers' daughters had a bad reputation
in Shakespeare's time. These themes of loss of virginity
and the end of love recur in Ophelia's song of St Valen-
tine's Day.

All this is accepted. Yet what Shakespeare scholars have
not noted is a medieval Welsh tale of a girl turned into an
owl as a punishment for sexual betrayal. This occurs in the
Four Branches of the Mabinogi. When the evil sorceress
Aranrhod declares her son Lleu shall have no human wife,
the magician Gwydion outwits her by creating a wife from
the flowers of oak, broom, and meadowsweet. He calls her
Blodeuedd 'flower queen'. She is fair but faithless, taking
a lover, Gronw, who tries to murder Lleu with a spear.
Lleu escapes by flying away as an eagle. When he is
restored to human form, Blodeuedd flees, but is caught

and punished by Gwydion, who turns her into an owl, declaring that birds will mob (*baedu*) and molest her wherever they find her. The author closes by saying this is why the owl is now called *Blodeuwedd* ('flower face').[3]

The tale of Blodeuedd was known to later writers. The fourteenth-century bard Dafydd ap Gwilym lists defects of a 'filthy' owl that disturbs his sleep, concluding:

> And her face, like that of a gentle human being,
> And her form, she-fiend of birds.
> Each unclean bird of alien kind
> Will harass (*baedd*) her; is it not strange she lives?

In her notes on this poem Rachel Bromwich suggests Dafydd alludes to the *Four Branches* tale of Blodeuedd, particularly as the uncommon verb *baeddu* occurs in both texts.[4] Since Dafydd's friend Rhydderch ab Ieuan commissioned the White Book of Rhydderch (oldest surviving manuscript of the *Four Branches*), this is no surprise. Dafydd had ample opportunity to read the tales at Rhydderch's house in West Wales.[5]

In another poem, formerly attributed to Dafydd (but probably of the fifteenth century), an owl scolds a poet, begging him to leave her alone in misery. She tells him,

> The nobles of unrivalled grace
> Called me Blodeuwedd, Flower-face.
> My father was son to Meirchion,
> And I, in truth, am sprung from Môn [Anglesey].

When the poet asks who changed her, she replies,

> Gwydion, the son of Don, with his wand,
> Of matchless power upon the sand
> Of Conwy, changed my loveliness
> To this thou seest, this bitterness;
> Gwydion of noble kin
> Because 'twas punishable sin
> To love the lord Gronw Pebyr
> Of Penllyn, son of Pefr Goronhir.[6]

This is effectively the *Four Branches* story, except that Blodeuedd is said to be of human origin and from Anglesey.[7]

How does this concern Ophelia? Both the tale of the baker's daughter and the *Four Branches* tell of a girl punished by being turned into an owl. Yet the Welsh story is older, and deals with sexual transgression and perfidy as the English one does not. Jackson warned against seeing myths of gods in the tale of Blodeuedd.[8] But the pagan Celts worshipped an owl-goddess; so Blodeuedd's transformation may derive from myth.[9]

In any case, there is reason to take the tale of the baker's daughter as ultimately Celtic. Its history may have been thus. In Welsh the girl's punishment follows betrayal in love, but that is lost sight of in our English versions. So Shakespeare may have heard the story in an earlier form, which described sexual deceit (like our second Welsh poem, found in sixteenth-century manuscripts).[10] It may be significant that Douce knew his tale from Gloucestershire, which borders Wales. The story in its original form would tell of love, betrayal, and a beautiful girl suffering a tragic fate, thus mirroring Ophelia's state of mind, as our English folklore versions do not.

Notes

1. *Hamlet*, 532–3.
2. Respectively A 1958.0.1 and D 153.2 in Thompson.
3. Jones and Jones, 74.
4. Dafydd ap Gwilym, *Selection*, 84, 99.
5. Breeze, *Medieval Welsh Literature*, 111.
6. Dafydd ap Gwilym, *Fifty Poems*, 283, 285.
7. Gruffydd, *Math*, 255; *Trioedd*, 456–7.
8. Jackson, *International Popular Tale*, 106–13.
9. Ross, 344–6.
10. *Peniarth 76*, 144–5.

The *Four Branches* in Our Time

What has discussion of the *Four Branches* from the early twentieth century until the present to reveal on their date and provenance? And, in particular, what have historians to say here? Though many writers have dealt with the *Four Branches*, the comments of historians (for whom the tales provide useful information on early Wales) are often neglected by literary scholars. Yet they should have special value, as concerning real events in real time. They may hence say more about the origins of these tales than do studies of their artistry and narrative technique (important though these are).

I

So we begin in 1911 with Sir John Lloyd (1861–1947), greatest of Welsh historians, whose vigorous patriotism was combined with scrupulous regard for fact. He referred to the *Four Branches* on matters of topography and politics. Citing other early references to the Roman fort of Segontium (outside modern Caernarfon, in north-west Wales), he noted how it was there that king Bendigeidfran was found (at an assembly) by the starling bearing a letter from his sister Branwen, telling of her ill-treatment in Ireland. Lloyd here noted appositely that Segontium's medieval importance was not merely legendary, the fort clearly being 'the ancient centre of the cantref' (=local adminstrative district), though it was later 'eclipsed' by Dolbadarn (six miles east of Segontium, below the slopes of Snowdon).[1] Lloyd also mentioned Harlech and Tomen-y-Mur (other royal sites in Gwynedd) in the *Four Branches*, as well as the mountains of Preseli in Dyfed, 'scene of many a romantic story', where 'the barons of the legendary King Pwyll met to expostulate with him upon the absence of an heir to the crown'.[2] Lloyd knew the lack of a heir to the throne is always a political matter, and not 'romantic' at all (as history both Welsh and Russian brings out). Pwyll's barons are civil but in earnest, inheritance in medieval Wales being a matter of political survival. Lloyd's citation elsewhere of this incident, on the clamour of Pwyll's men against a marriage that after three years had brought no heir (they demand that he divorce Rhiannon and marry another), clarifies the political implications of the incident and underlines the political realism of the *Four Branches*.[3] Lloyd's understanding of statecraft is something one would expect from him. But the author of the *Four Branches* also had a grasp of these matters (as recent scholars have emphasized). This is more surprising. We shall return to this point.

Lloyd also thought the date of the *Mabinogion* worth mentioning. He described the evidence as limited, but tended to link the stories with the age of Llywelyn the Great (d. 1240).[4] Though nobody now accepts this, it is to Lloyd's credit that he thought the origins of these 'famous romantic tales' still merited serious historical attention.

II

A contrast to Lloyd's comments is provided by W. J. Gruffydd (1881–1954). He was an unlikely combination of poet and mythologist (with a special interest in magic), who ended his career in the House of Commons as MP for the University of Wales (a seat abolished long ago). His investigations, though extensive, say almost nothing on when and where the *Four Branches* were written.[5] For further discussion we have to turn to Sir Ifor Williams

(1881–1965). He attributed them to a Dyfed author who also used material from Gwynedd and Gwent (south-east Wales). He thought the likeliest date for this was about 1060, when almost the whole of Wales was united under the rule of Gruffudd ap Llywelyn (d. 1063). This he considered preferable to Joseph Loth's 1889 suggestion of the later twelfth century; or Alfred Nutt's (in 1910) of the period when Gruffudd ap Cynan was king of Gwynedd (1075–1137) and Rhys ap Tewder was king of Dyfed (1070–93).[6] Although Williams's reasoning is hardly compelling, his commanding authority as a scholar meant his opinions would be echoed for many years.

Published after Ifor Williams's great edition of the *Four Branches*, but sent to press too early to make use of it, the views of the Chadwicks show independent thinking. With Cambridge common sense, they tended to discount the mythological element in the *Mabinogi*. They pointed out how little the characters and incidents have in common with supposed equivalents in Irish mythological texts, and how in any case the characters are represented as human beings, not gods and goddesses. They discussed in detail the first and last branches, observing that Pwyll is a 'typical heroic prince of the better sort', with no magic powers. They did not regard his story as heroic: 'he himself either plays a purely passive role or acts as he is directed'. They conclude that the tale is purely one of 'entertainment'. Yet, as regards the story of Math, they nevertheless emphasize the magic powers of the ruling family of Gwynedd, the heroic element being secondary.[7]

Sir Ifor Williams's splendid edition of the *Four Branches* had the unfortunate effect (like other magisterial scholarship) of sedating discussion rather than provoking it. As regards historians a rare alternative view was provided by A. H. Williams's summary of Sir John Lloyd's history. He cautiously referred to supposed Scandinavian origins for the tale of Branwen (as argued in Timothy Lewis's 1931 book *Mabinogi Cymru*: a literary still-birth), perhaps through the influence of Gruffudd ap Cynan, who had links with the Norse of Dublin.[8] Though the historical context is reasonable, the literary evidence is lacking. No philologist has accepted this view.

What was effectively Gruffydd's last comment on the *Four Branches* came in his posthumous study *Rhiannon*. He there spoke of composition 'before the end of the eleventh century', accepting the evidence of language and orthography set out by Ifor Williams. On the place of composition he was more cautious. Although the dialect of the *Four Branches* had been seen as that of Dyfed, Gruffydd thought we did not know enough of Middle Welsh dialects to be sure here. As regards place-names, he thought the texts showed greater familiarity with Gwynedd than with Dyfed, though he also thought the evidence here was inconclusive.[9]

III

In an important survey, Rachel Bromwich (1915–) follows Ifor Williams in dating the *Four Branches* to the later eleventh century, and seeing their redactor as a professional story-teller from South Wales, there being traces of South Wales dialect in the orthography of the texts.[10] (We shall dispute almost almost all of this below.) Sir Thomas Parry (1904–1985) made the judicious comment in his standard history of Welsh literature that some suppose the *Four Branches* were put together about 1060, though others consider feudal references would put them later (so that Teyrnon, a lord of Gwent in the first branch, is described as Pwyll's former *gwr* 'man; vassal'). But Parry declared all agree the tales are the work of a single author, 'a writer of the most brilliant kind'.[11] He saw no reason whatever to divide the stories up amongst two or more writers. His forthrightness here should be noted, since the point is still disputed by writers in Wales and the USA.

In a convenient edition of the first branch, Robert Thomson (formerly of Leeds University) follows Ifor Williams in dating the tales to the late eleventh century, though not necessarily to the reign of Gruffudd ap

Llywelyn (1055–63), since there would always have been 'free trade in stories, more especially as there was a class of *kyuarwydyeit* or storytellers to foster it'. He thinks the stories were probably edited in the south, although a good deal of the matter concerns people in north-west Wales.[12]

In a major study of Irish elements in the second branch, Proinsias Mac Cana (1926–2004) made some innovative suggestions. He thought likely a connection with Gruffudd ap Cynan, a Gwynedd king who had strong links with Ireland, where he was born and where he spent periods of exile. However, Mac Cana tended to see the second branch in particular as 'a work composed and written in the study', its author being 'almost certainly a scholar' in a monastic community, like the authors of much early Irish saga. He went further to suggest the author may have been Sulien (1011–1091), sometime Bishop of St Davids, or his son Rhygyfarch (1056/7–99), author of a Latin life of St David.[13] Mac Cana was later more cautious on this matter, as we shall see below.

Some penetrating comments were made by K. H. Jackson (1909–1991), greatest of all English Celticists. He rejected outright the view that the *Four Branches* were composed by a professional storyteller. Such a person would not have been responsible for the many incoherences of plot in the tales. Jackson's opinion carries weight, since he had first-hand experience in the 1930s of recording material from professional storytellers in the west of Ireland. He thus regarded the *Four Branches* as the composition of a gifted amateur, living at a court of high status (not a monastery). He felt that the familiarity of the tales with the life of Welsh kings and nobles makes this ambience quite clear.[14]

Professor Derick Thomson (1921–) of Glasgow, in contrast, follows the lead of Gruffydd and Mac Cana. He describes the *Four Branches* as made up of very diverse sources, 'finally welded and moulded by an editor who may have been a cleric whose moralistic and satirical tendencies are generally, but not always, submerged by his ambition to tell a good story well.' He sets down the opinion that the author came from Dyfed and was active in the later eleventh century.[15]

In a curious study of Welsh religious thought in ancient and medieval times, Pennar Davies drew attention to the troubled picture of invasion given in the third branch, with Caswallon's occupation of Britain and the journey of Pryderi of Dyfed to Oxford to become his vassal, which he compared with the condition of Wales in the age of Gruffydd ap Llywelyn (1055–63).[16] The same dating is accepted by Ceri Lewis, who echoes Ifor Williams's view that the *Four Branches* were assembled by a man of Dyfed, who used traditions from Gwynedd, Dyfed, and Gwent about 1060, 'when these three kingdoms had been politically united by Gruffudd ap Llywelyn'.[17]

An important survey of opinion on the *Four Branches of the Mabinogi* was given by the late Professor Jarman of Cardiff. He noted Joseph Loth's opinion of 1913 that they were later than the Norman Conquest of 1066, but earlier than about 1150. (This contasts with Loth's view of 1889, cited above, that all eleven *Mabinogion* tales were of the later twelfth century.) In 1913 W. J. Gruffydd had also expressed the much stranger hypothesis that the first branch dated to about 1000, the second to about 1050, the third to about 1150, and the last to about 1160 (so that they could not possibly be by the same author). One notes Gruffydd retreated from this bizarre opinion in his later writings. In a series of articles of 1969–70, the poet and patriot Saunders Lewis (1893–1985), whose views on Welsh literature were sometimes to the point, sometimes not, proposed in that the *Four Branches* may have been written by a Cistercian monk of Strata Florida (near Aberystwyth, in mid-Wales) about 1170–90. No scholar has accepted this. Jarman also cited the more sober opinion of Thomas Charles-Edwards of Oxford for a dating of the tales, on the basis of their allusions to feudalism, to between 1050 and 1120.[18]

In the first edition of his booklet on the subject, Proinsias Mac Cana rightly commented on the dangers of 'a received, conformist appraisal of these works', and welcomed recent challenges to 'the virtual monopoly of one or two authoritative scholars' on them. After citing the views of Saunders Lewis and Charles-Edwards, he thus concluded that their dating was 'still very much an open question'.[19]

Morfydd Owen of Aberystwyth has perceptive comments on the second branch, the tale of Branwen. Her use of this text in a collection of essays on women and medieval Welsh law again underlines the value of the *Four Branches* for historians. Worth noting here is her comment that these texts 'have proved themselves a rich repository for students of early Welsh society'. She adds that Branwen's status, as a Welsh princess married to an Irish king, sheds much light on the relations of different kin-groups; the tale also makes constant use of legal concepts and vocabulary as regards honour-price, or compensation for *sarhaed* ('insult'), such as the cutting-off by Bendigeidfran's half-brother Efnisien of the lips, ears, tails, and eyelids of the Irish king's horses.[20] These and other aspects of the narratives show their author's practical knowledge of law and legal processes, especially as regards diplomacy, royal status, and the settlement of disputes.

In striking contrast to the above is a comment on the *Four Branches* from the late A. J. Taylor, a Chief Inspector of Ancient Monuments and (in 1975–8) President of the Society of Antiquaries, London. In a pamphlet on Harlech Castle he quoted the opening of the second branch, describing Bendigeidfran and his court 'on the rock of Harlech overlooking the sea', when they saw the fleet of the King of Ireland approching them. Taylor, who referred to the text as 'mythology', noted how in May 1283 (when Edward I instigated work on the castle) Harlech emerged 'from the realms of folk-tale and myth into the light of recorded fact'.[21] Taylor knew no Welsh and had little interest in Welsh tradition. His comments, which one might well call retrograde, show the dangers of received opinion. It should be emphasized that the *Four Branches*, far from being mere 'myth', reveal much about government, politics, and military organization from the viewpoint of the Welsh ruling class. One must also protest against Taylor's dismissive and patronizing expression 'folk-tale'. The *Four Branches* are not 'folk-tales' as work of the 'folk'. They are art which is aristocratic to the core. Taylor's comments serve a useful function as revealing unthinking attitudes to the *Mabinogion* which persist even in educated circles, especially outside Wales.

Professor Wendy Davies of London University has some cautious remarks on the *Four Branches*. She notes the disagreements of both historians and philologists on their dating, though she thinks in their present form they surely belong to the century after 1066, while the Normans were beginning their conquest of Wales. She comments further on disagreements as regards their authorship. Some see them as a 'fusion of different elements of different provenance'; others as 'conscious literary creations' with 'organic unity'; a third group stresses the disparate element within them. The whole question of dating and provenance remains 'extremely complex'.[22] Though a historian, Professor Davies hence refrains from categorical views on this text.

Some perceptive comments on popular narrative were made by Juliette Wood in 1985. These are of special interest in the present context. She points out that the heroines Rhiannon and Branwen differ in character. Nevertheless, they both marry into alien communities, and there both suffer persecution after marriage. She refers to anthropological and other discussion of this common folklore motif, as well as to evidence from medieval Welsh law.[23] She does not pause to consider whether the use of such a motif not once but twice might correspond to personal concerns of the author, for whom the situation of a royal bride who marries outside her kin (thereby becoming an outsider within her husband's community) was clearly a matter of interest.

Professor R. R. Davies (1938–2005) of Oxford, a Welshman in many ways writing (with full emphasis on native sources) in the tradition of Sir John Lloyd, made copious references to the *Four Branches*. He naturally paid attention to their comments on politics, government, and society. He also referred to Gwenllian, to her father Gruffudd ap Cynan, and to her husband Gruffydd ap Rhys (though, of course, with no suspicion whatsoever that Gwenllian might be very closely related indeed to the *Four Branches*). Let us set down some of his remarks. He quoted the native Welsh chronicles on Gruffydd's rising of 1116, with its aim of 'repairing and renewing the British kingdom'. Exactly the same aim for the principality of Dyfed appears in the *Mabinogi* (where Dyfed by the fourth branch has expanded to cover almost all southern Wales). Davies, writing from a nationalist viewpoint, observes how the 'native prose tales, notably the *Mabinogi*, assume an audience that can move freely in its imagination across the whole of Wales'. (This opinion contrasts with that quoted below of Brynley Roberts, who observes how unusual the *Four Branches* are in placing their action in different parts of Wales. The oddness of this strikes Dr Roberts, but not Professor Davies.) Davies commented further on the intimate knowledge of Wales's administrative geography shown by these stories; their awareness of the royal *cylch* or circuit (historically often little more than legalized pillage), on which Pwyll goes; their depiction of royal councils, where kings hear the advice of their nobles, to which they are in many ways bound; feudal practices, as when Matholwch in the second branch sues for peace with Bendigeidfran, and renders the sovereignty of Ireland to him; the emphasis in the first branch on Arawn's wise, generous, and just rule of Dyfed; and the intimate famil- iarity of the stories with matters of formal public repara- tion for insults to honour (as with the mutilation of Matholwch's horses). Finally, Professor Davies on facing pages comments on the leading roles of some Welsh- women. In January 1136, Amazonian Gwenllian led troops into attack on the Normans at Kidwelly, by the coast of southern Wales; Rhiannon makes the devastating riposte to her suitor Pwyll, 'Never did man make worse use of his wits than thou hast done.'[24] The possibility that Gwenllian actually composed Rhiannon's words would no doubt have greatly surprised Professor Davies. (One wonders what he would say to it.) If she did, these two Welsh-women would be linked more closely than he imagined. In a wide-ranging paper, John Koch of Aberystwyth relates aspects of the *Four Branches* to ancient Celtic tradition in pre-Roman Britain and in archaic Irish sources. With reason, he emphasizes parts of the *Four Branches* that show a concern for moral and political authority.[25] This point is significant and has rightly been developed by later commentators, as we shall see. It confirms the interest shown in these tales by historians of Wales from the days of Sir John Lloyd, but reacts against the obsession with mythology of some earlier scholars. Developing arguments set out by Kenneth Jackson, Andrew Welsh of Rutgers University in this context provides a useful analysis of the 230 folklore motifs in these four stories, of which he regards about eighty per cent as 'international' and the remainder as 'Celtic'.[26] Such a conclusion tends to undermine the case of those stressing the 'mythological' and 'Celtic' aspect of the tales. It places them rather within the great international tradition of storytelling, extending from Iceland and Spain to Russia, India, and beyond.

Marie Flanagan, noting that the *Four Branches* are dated to between the eleventh and thirteenth centuries, discusses the palace of wattles (stakes interlaced with twigs and branches to make walls and so on) that the Irish kings built in Dublin for Henry II at Christmas 1171 (where he received their submission). Such temporary feasting-houses often figure in early Irish sources, like *Bricriu's Feast* or the metrical *Dindshenchas* (where they contrast with the tents used by Welsh rulers in the *Mabinogi*). Palaces of twigs and branches are paralleled in the second branch by the hall that Matholwch built to conciliate Bendigeidfran. Marie Flanagan does not, however, propose that Henry II's visit inspired the account in the tale of Branwen. She also refers, quite separately, to the military activities and Irish connections of Gruffudd ap Cynan (d. 1137) of Gwynedd and Gruffydd ap Rhys (d. 1137) of Dyfed, and even to Gwenllian's fatal attack in 1136 on Kidwelly.[27]

In another paper on the first branch, Andrew Welsh considers the *Mabinogi*'s notorious defects of construction and plot, which Jackson thought proved it could not possibly be the work of a professional storyteller. (This view would make irrevelant much recent discussion of their role in the telling of these tales.) Citing the work of the North American writers J. K. Bollard, Catherine McKenna, and Jeffrey Ganz, Welsh takes a more positive view of these narrative matters. He calls the *Mabinogi* a 'work of coherent artistry', since it treats questions of friendship, love, marriage, loyalty, and good counsel (as also enmity, deceit, and treachery) with a unity of vision. He thus stresses its moral, social, and even political coherence.[28] This is an attractive, welcome, and convincing case. It is part of a continued move away from unconvincing attempts by earlier writers to extract a supposed original glorious mythological narrative from the ruins of it discerned in the *Mabinogi*. The older view that the author had wonderful material, but did not understand it and so told it badly, hardly explains why millions of readers have found these stories so artistically satisfying. It is more intelligent and mature to show us the creative perfection and moral integrity of the narratives as we have them (rather than hunt for some allegedly more splendid lost original that they preserve in scraps). This helps explain the supremely high place that the *Mabinogi* enjoys in world literature, as earlier theories do not.

In a later study, Wendy Davies notes that the Irish connections of the tale of Branwen can be related to much other evidence for Welsh-Irish contacts in the eleventh and twelfth centuries.[29] Kari Maund of Cardiff observes in passing that the years of poverty which king Gruffudd ap Cynan (d. 1137) passed in Gwynedd on his return from exile resemble those of Manawydan in the third branch of the *Mabinogi*.[30] Since we argue that Gruffudd's daughter wrote these stories, no surprise. Irish connections are also considered by Patrick Sims-Williams of Aberystwyth, who

concludes that the house that the Irish built for Bendigei-
dran in the second branch sheds no light on its date, and
quotes Mac Cana for the view that dating is 'still very
much an open question'.[31]

In a collection of essays, Brynley Roberts (1931–),
formerly of the National Library of Wales, Aberystwyth,
makes varied remarks on the *Mabinogi,* where he describes
the text as of 'the period 1050–1120'. His views here are
more conservative and less incisive than some in his more
recent writings, to which we shall return.[32] In a study of
early Welsh law, Huw Pryce of Bangor cites two passages
from the *Mabinogi* (which he dates to between the late
eleventh and early thirteenth century). When in the third
branch the heroine Cigfa finds herself alone with
Manawydan, and fears she will be raped, he swears he
will treat her honourably, saying 'I give thee God for
surety (*mach*) that thou hast not seen a comrade truer than
thou wilt find me.' Pryce notes this instance of giving God
as surety is paralleled in early Roman and Irish law, but is
unknown in Germanic law except in the laws of Alfred,
where it may be due to Welsh influence, perhaps thanks to
Bishop Asser (d. 909), Alfred's Welsh biographer.[33] Whitelock observed of it there that it would be used by those
(like traders) with no kindred at hand to act as surety.[34] As
Cigfa and Manawydan are in a wilderness, his use of it is
apt. It thus shows how precise was the Welsh author's
knowledge of native law. Pryce comments further on incidents in the first branch, where Pwyll's nobles petition
him to divorce Rhiannon because she has borne him no
children (he asks them for respite till the end of a year).
Pryce concludes from this that in early Wales a husband
might repudiate his wife for childlessness.[35]

In a full-length study of medieval Welsh narrative, the
work of many years, Professor Sioned Davies of Cardiff
gives what might even now be called received opinion in
the University of Wales. Most regard the *Four Branches* as
having one author only. After reviewing opinions by Ifor
Williams, Joseph Loth, Morgan Watkin (of Bangor), Saunders Lewis, and Thomas Charles-Edwards for datings

between about 1060 and 1250, she quotes Sims-Williams and Mac Cana for the view that dating is 'still very much an open question'. She observes further that this makes it difficult to place the tales in any historical or social context. As regards authorship, she quotes Mac Cana's 1958 attribution of them to Bishop Sulien (1011–1091) of St Davids or his son Rhygyfarch (1056/7–99). But she notes how Mac Cana in the revised 1992 edition of his *The Mabinogi* here admitted faults in his original methodology.[36] In short, little that is certain.

It will be seen from the above that the professor of Celtic at Aberystwyth and the professor of Welsh at Cardiff cannot say within the widest limits when the *Four Branches* were written. (D. R. Johnston, professor of Welsh at Swansea, also informed the writer at Galway in July 2004 that he could not say exactly when these stories were composed.) After generations of work, professors within Wales are thus less certain on this matter than ever.

However, a fresh approach was provided in 1997 by Fiona Winward, who considers at length the question of gender in the *Four Branches*, though making no conclusions on the question of their date and provenance.[37] Siân Echard of the University of British Columbia, Canada, also looks at the *Four Branches* with freshness and originality. She sees tart satire in the first branch, referring to Pwyll's curious and persistent obtuseness there (she calls him 'rather dim'), so that even his betrothed wife Rhiannon castigates his foolishness. As *Pwyll* means 'sense, wisdom', the author's irony is surely conscious and evident. But there is more than that. Siân Echard points out that Pwyll must learn wisdom as a ruler, a concern with good government running through all four of these narratives (here she cites a study of 1981–2 by Elizabeth Hanson-Smith). She goes so far as to call the *Four Branches* a 'mirror for princes' predating similar works by Latin court writers of the twelfth century. She considers this would accord with the attribution by Rachel Bromwich of these tales to a lawyer, or at least someone in touch with the Welsh tradition of legal prose. Here we may add to this by placing this Welsh concern with good government beside words of Hildebert of Lavardin (1056–1133) to the count of Anjou (quoted by Sir Richard Southern) on 'the innate dignity of the secular order of society'.[38] Siân Echard thus adds to the sustained emphasis amongst literary scholars since the early 1980s on the informed knowledge of politics that these stories provide, as also their concern with good government. As Southern makes clear, the latter was a subject receiving new attention in the early decades of the twelfth century.

In 1999 Laurie Finke, in a sober and clearly written study of writing by medieval women, gave a careful account of the present writer's views on the authorship of the *Four Branches*, though she considers lack of evidence makes it impossible to disprove this case.[39] In the same year Ian Hughes of Aberystwyth wrote a somewhat old-fashioned piece, based in many respects on the work of W. J. Gruffydd, and concluding that the theme of the fourth branch is not that in which the King's death is foretold (as Gruffydd maintained), but rather that of the controlling activities of the sorcerer Gwydion.[40] Also in 1999 Catherine McKenna, now of Harvard, wrote on Manawydan, whom she regards as offering, like Pwyll, 'a model of effective sovereignty for an age in which shrewdness, circumspection, and accommodation were essential instruments of good governance'.[41] But she says nothing on the dating and origin of these narratives.

IV

We may conclude with five recent studies, which show the question of date and provenance as much in the air as ever, or at least as showing the lack of unanimity amongst commentators. First, Brynley Roberts. In a paper of major importance, he comes to some clear conclusions about the *Four Branches*. He thinks they were written in Gwynedd, and perhaps at the ancient Celtic monastery of Clynnog, a small place by the sea some thirteen miles south of

Caernarfon in north-west Wales. Roberts cites Sims-Williams for Clynnog as 'a strong candidate on both cultural and geographical grounds'. That is dubious. This writer thinks, in contast, that the case for Clynnog is one of singular feebleness. Yet we may readily agree on Roberts's other conclusions regarding the *Four Branches*: that they are a single work in four parts; that they have a 'dual geography', uniquely locating their narrative in both north and south Wales; and that they show the 'hand and voice of a single author'. Roberts goes on to find their unity in a consistent concern with good government, which is a moral question as well as a political one. He firmly discards the quest by Gruffydd and others for some glorious mythological saga (dimly reflected in what we now have) as a hunt for a mare's nest. All must agree this represents considerable progress. Finally, Roberts mentions without acceptance or rejection this writer's views on the authorship of the *Four Branches*.[42]

Four other papers may be dealt with more briefly. In a paper dated to 2002 (but appearing in the summer of 2004), the independent scholar William Parker discusses in detail the present writer's arguments on Gwenllian and the *Mabinogi*, which he describes as 'attractive', although he notes that some would regard them as inconclusive.[43] For all its originality, it must be said that Parker's paper is not always accurate in its geography (as in its otherwise useful map of *Mabinogi* locations). Three other papers discuss recent work on these texts (without reference to the present writer). Paul Russell of Cambridge reviews the work of Brynley Roberts and Patrick Sims-Williams on the question, noting their tendency to see the *Four Branches* as written in Gwynedd (not Dyfed), and associating them with the ancient Celtic religious community at Clynnog, near Caernarfon.[44] Catherine McKenna continues her investigations into the political aspects of the fourth branch, and its concerns with good government.[45] Finally, Ned Sturzer, an independent scholar of Chattanooga, Tennessee, boldly advances the opinion that the narrative inconsistencies of our four tales mean no two of them can be regarded as by the same author. He says nothing on the dating or exact provenance of any one of these branches.[46] His arguments on the non-integrity of the *Four Branches*, which fly in the face of work by Thomas Parry, Brynley Roberts, and other Welsh scholars, are not compelling. Few readers are likely to see different hands in either the style of these stories or their representation of character. Nor need the contradictions of the narrative be taken to show different redactors at work. Many great literary works contain such contradictions. Obvious examples occur in Shakespeare. We are told Hamlet is a student at Wittenberg, but later discover that he is thirty; Lady Macbeth speaks of having had children, whom we hear no more of; but no scholar will argue that these contradictions show that Shakespeare was not the effective sole author of *Hamlet* or *Macbeth*. Where Shakespeare did have a co-author (as in the first part of *Pericles*), the style makes this obvious. One can hardly point to such contrasts or disparities of style in the *Mabinogi*.

We may go further with examples that will be familiar in Russia (where Shakespeare has been so long admired and well translated) from *Henry IV* and *The Merry Wives of Windsor*. Here we may quote comments made by Professor Craik of Durham. 'Mistress Quickly's circumstances in *The Merry Wives of Windsor*, where she is Dr Caius's housekeeper, is unmarried, and has to introduce herself to Falstaff, are quite different from those in 1 and 2 *Henry IV*, where she is the married (in 2 *Henry IV* widowed) hostess of a London tavern and has known Falstaff for nearly thirty years.'[47] Ned Sturzer might conclude from such inconsistencies that *Henry IV* and *The Merry Wives of Windsor* could not be by the same author. That would be going wrong with confidence. The answer must be that narrative consistency (as we might find it in the fiction of Trollope or Galsworthy) did not trouble Shakespeare, or his public. Examples can also be found in a writer who is Shakespeare's equal. In *War and Peace*, Natasha appears in 1805 as a child of thirteen; in 1809 she is sixteen. Her sister is seventeen in 1805 and twenty-four in 1809. Nikolai

Rostov joins the army in September 1805 and returns in February 1806. Yet in the memorable account of his homecoming we are told he has been away 'a year and a half'. Kutuzov is said to have only one eye, but Tolstoy still mentions his 'eyes'. Prince Andrei's sister Maria puts round his neck a silver icon on a silver chain; when he is picked up wounded on the battlefield, the French remove from his neck a gold icon on a gold chain, placed there by Princess Maria.[48] Yet no reader will think such inconsistencies suggest *War and Peace* is not by one author.

Enough has been done to show that the *Mabinogi* is at present receiving more critical attention than ever. The mass (even 'ferment') of material thus provides unusual opportunities for research. This is especially the case when there is no agreement even on matters so simple as the date and provenance of these tales, despite the wealth of topographical, social, and political information they contain. There is clearly room for a study that will sift out what is of permanent value from what is not. Then we shall see more clearly the *Four Branches of the Mabinogi*, the greatest part of the *Mabinogion*, a collection of tales which are Wales's most precious gift to the literature of the world.

Notes

1. Lloyd, *History*, 234–5.
2. Lloyd, *History*, 238–9, 263.
3. Lloyd, *History*, 291 n. 36.
4. Lloyd, *History*, 692.
5. Gruffydd, *Math, passim*.
6. *Pedeir Keinc*, xxxvii-xli.
7. Chadwick and Chadwick, 114–16.
8. A. H. Williams, 154.
9. Gruffydd, *Rhiannon*, 6–7.
10. Bromwich, 'Character', 102.
11. Parry, 70.
12. *Pwyll*, xvi.
13. Mac Cana, *Branwen*, 180–7.

14. Jackson, *International Popular Tale*, 124–30.
15. *Branwen*, xxx-xxxi.
16. Pennar Davies, 105.
17. C. W. Lewis, 456.
18. Jarman, *'Pedair Keinc y Mabinogi'*, 87–8.
19. Mac Cana, *Mabinogi*, 21–4.
20. Owen, 'Shame', 58–60.
21. Taylor, 4.
22. Wendy Davies, *Wales*, 211–12.
23. Wood, 25–38.
24. R. R. Davies, 16, 17–18, 20, 21, 64, 69–70, 74–5, 77, 116–17, 128, 129.
25. Koch, 17–52.
26. Welsh, 'Traditional Narrative Motifs', 51–62.
27. Flanagan, *Irish Society*, 64, 67, 140, 204–5.
28. Welsh, 'Traditional Tales', 15–41.
29. Wendy Davies, *Patterns*, 40.
30. Maund, *Ireland, Wales, and England*, 177.
31. Sims-Williams, 'Submission', 31–61.
32. Roberts, *Studies*, 96.
33. Pryce, 63, 92–3.
34. *English Historical Documents*, 413.
35. Pryce, 92–3.
36. Sioned Davies, 7–8.
37. Winward, 77–106.
38. Southern, *Making*, 95; Echard, 196–7, 200–1.
39. Finke, 103–4.
40. Hughes, 9–21.
41. McKenna, 'Education', 101–30.
42. Roberts, 'Where Were the *Four Branches of the Mabinogi* Written?', 61–75.
43. Parker, 365–96.
44. Russell, 'Recent Work', 59–72.
45. McKenna, 'Revising Math', 95–117.
46. Sturzer, 127–42.
47. *Merry Wives*, 11–12.
48. Tolstoy, xv-xvi.

Where the *Four Branches* were Written

Internet bibliographies show the *Four Branches of the Mabinogi* attract growing attention, especially in North America: a proper tribute to their excellence. Yet they still pose problems of interpretation. So much is shown by a recent paper of Brynley Roberts, where he argues that the *Four Branches* were written in Gwynedd, and perhaps at Clynnog (in the Lleyn Peninsula), which he calls 'a strong candidate on both cultural and geographical grounds'.[1] Such views demand a reply. What follows thus falls into two parts, with the first summarizing Roberts's case, and the second responding to it. One may say at once that this matter concerns historians as well as philologists, because the *Four Branches* are not just a literary text. Sir John Lloyd continually cited them for historical information, and this practice is rightly continued by R. R. Davies in his Oxford *History of Wales* volume.[2] If, then, the *Four Branches* can be accurately dated, provenanced, and (ideally) provided with an author, their historical value will be increased. Historians will be able to use their depiction of early Welsh politics and society with confidence, knowing they are precisely located in time and space.

I

Brynley Roberts begins his survey with a comment on the uniqueness of the *Four Branches*. Much in them has no equivalent in other Welsh literature, as in (for example) their use of *ceinc* 'branch' as a term for a story. He cites Ceri Lloyd-Morgan on the parallel between this and *branche* 'branch' in French narratives from about 1150.[3] But he tends to agree with her that the *Four Branches* predate that, so that the parallel would be coincidental. He notes that the *Four Branches* are also remarkable in locating narratives in both north and south Wales. They are 'firmly set in both Gwynedd and Dyfed'. They also place a rare emphasis on processes of government. These include the territorial expansion of Dyfed; the diplomatic and even military relationships of Gwynedd and Dyfed, Gwynedd and Penllyn, and Dyfed and Gwent; and the grant to Lleu Llaw Gyffes of Dinoding (=Eifionydd and Ardudwy, north-east of Cardigan Bay). They say much of royal courts. Pwyll has one at Arberth (near Cardigan), Pryderi another at Rhuddlan Teifi (near Lampeter), while Bran the Blessed holds court at Harlech, Caer Seint (near Caernarfon), Aberffraw, and Caer Dathyl in Arfon. Roberts correctly describes this emphasis on the mechanics of government as 'unusual'.

He then points out that the texts are 'the most clearly authored' of all native Welsh stories. Modern critics no longer follow Matthew Arnold in seeing them as the work of a folk narrator, ineptly reassembling pre-Christian narratives; or of Kenneth Jackson, who saw them as the work of an antiquarian, putting together half-forgotten mythological tales.[4] Roberts makes the penetrating and fundamental observation that, since we do not know what those sources were, we can hardly say how they were used. On the personality of the author, he says the texts avoid conventional modes of chivalry, hero-tale, propaganda, or folktale, though they are closer to contemporary romance than to traditional storytelling. Nevertheless, they give the impression of a personal and distinctive vision of life, love, and death in early Wales. Perhaps no other Welsh writer has described so well the joys and sorrows of human existence: nothing in these stories is predictable or hackneyed.

Having outlined the special features of the *Four*

Branches (a single work in four parts; a dual geography; and the 'hand and voice of a single author'), Roberts turns to the question of their unity. Edward Anwyl and W. J. Gruffydd saw the birth, life, and death of Pryderi as the thread that links the tales; Ifor Williams, though lacking respect for Gruffydd's speculations, still followed him on this point. Running through the minds of all three scholars was the notion of the *Four Branches* as shattered relics of a saga about Pryderi. But Roberts notes the scepticism here of recent critics, including P. K. Ford, Proinsias Mac Cana, and Andrew Welsh. They admire the *Four Branches* for what they are, rather than as a flawed version of some hypothetic earlier narrative, which is now almost lost (though supposedly leaving clues for adept literary archaeologists). Again, reasonable commentators will agree with Roberts that progress has been made here.

More provocative are his following remarks. Previous critics have seen the tales as Dyfed compositions, in part from a belief that Pryderi is their hero. Anwyl spoke as early as 1897 of their 'Dimetian bias' and Ifor Williams agreed, citing their warmth of reference to Dyfed ('there are not seven cantrefs better than they') and the sympathy they show for the men of Dyfed on the death of their leader, Pryderi. Yet Roberts calls this 'unconvincing'. He thinks the first comment (if 'more than a rhetorical commonplace') is bait to persuade Manawydan to marry Rhiannon, now past her prime, and a way of underlining the contrast with the magic wasting of Dyfed. As for the reference to the grief of the men of the south, it 'can equally well be read as triumphalism on the part of the men of Gwynedd. It is, in any event, a curious way to report the death of a Dyfed hero at mid-point in a Dyfed text'. (Some will regard all this as special pleading.) He argues that the Dyfed aspect of the tales is less important than that of Gwynedd; that they cannot be construed as a history of the misfortunes of Pryderi, as Anwyl thought; and that the protagonists are not the royal house of Dyfed, but that of Gwynedd. 'Throughout the Four Branches the priority of Gwynedd is emphasized.'

Roberts states further that the 'Gwynedd place-names in the text are more meaningful' and have 'a greater ring of confidence than the Dyfed locations'. He observes that Arberth, Preseleu, Llwyn Diarwya, and Glyn Cuch 'give no real sense of geography' (this is dubious), while the mythical associations of Gwales and Aberhenfelen matter more than their actual whereabouts; they lack the sense of a place visited and known that is clear for Aber Menei, Harlech, Aberffraw, or for the journey from Creuwyrion (near Bangor) to Caer Dathyl (near Caernarfon). The geography of Arfon is referred to 'with far greater assurance' than that of Dyfed is. Rejecting the hypothesis of multiple authorship, Brynley Roberts hence thinks the tales were written in Gwynedd.

He defends this view by reference to Gwynedd's literary history, with instances in archbishop Elfoddw (d. 809), *Historia Gruffudd ap Cynan* (a thirteenth-century translation of a lost Latin original), and early court poetry, including that of Hywel ab Owain Gwynedd (d. 1170). In this mileu the *Four Branches*, which he significantly describes as concerned with 'questions of wise governorship', might find a natural audience. He closes with the comment that he cannot say where in Gwynedd they might be written, but thinks Clynnog a 'strong candidate'; when they were written he thinks an 'open question', though he believes techniques of linguistic analysis may one day provide absolute dating for Middle Welsh texts. Yet he allows that, if *Culhwch and Olwen* was composed about 1100, the *Four Branches* are surely later, though probably earlier than about 1200.[5] If so, the parallel of *ceinc* and Old French *branche* might be relevant. (Roberts does not consider the point that, if the *Four Branches* were written much after the 1130s, it is strange they show no proven influence from Geoffrey of Monmouth's *History of the Kings of Britain*, published in 1136–1138 and achieving immediate fame.) However, Roberts is careful to observe that the fragments of the *Four Branches* in MS Peniarth 6, now thought to date from soon before 1300 (and not about 1225, as once believed), are not from Gwynedd. He thus admits the curious circumstance that, although he regards the *Four Branches* as composed in Gwynedd, the earliest manuscripts of them are from southern Wales.

This ends the summary of Brynley Roberts's case. Little in it can be disputed in terms of fact: much can be readily subscribed to. But there is a great deal one can disagree with as regards interpretation. The second part of this paper hence takes the information set out by Roberts, showing how his data may be used to provide a very different conclusion. The crucial question here is the representation of Dyfed and Gwynedd in the stories. Roberts's argument is as follows. Early scholarship saw Pryderi (a Dyfed ruler) as hero of the text; it was thus thought that the texts were written in Dyfed. Yet, as modern scholarship rejects Pryderi's central role, the case for Dyfed provenance collapses. This hence allows an origin in Gwynedd, as we might in any case deduce from the sharper focus of the tales on Gwynedd's topography and political power.

II

The problem here is the validity of the premises, not the logic of the reasoning. It means that Roberts has to decry Dyfed to strengthen the case for Gwynedd. This leads to five apparent misinterpretations. First, he says that the comment in the fourth branch on the sorrow of the men of Dyfed 'can equally well be read as triumphalism on the part of the men of Gwynedd'. Few readers will accept his 'equally well'. Let us look again at the passage. 'The men of the South (*Gwyr y Deheu*) set forth with bitter lamentation towards their own land. Nor was this strange. They had lost their lord, and many of their noblemen, and their horses, and their arms for the most part.'[6] And it is followed by the request from a Gwynedd hero that a noble Dyfed hostage be released from durance (this is at once granted), so that he and other hostages may follow their comrades south. It is hard to see 'triumphalism' in this. It is also hard to see why the author should include this humane reference to the vanquished except as a gesture to Dyfed feelings. But why should any author writing in Gwynedd for a Gwynedd audience feel a need to do that?

Second, Roberts says that it would be curious 'to report the death of a Dyfed hero at mid-point in a Dyfed text'. But that assumes the *Four Branches* are either purely Dyfed texts or purely Gwynedd ones. Inflexibility on this point will lead to error. The point can be made by looking at modern writing. How misleading such an approach would be if the work of Joseph Conrad (Polish or British?), T. S. Eliot (American or British?), or Samuel Beckett (Irish or French?) had been written in the Middle Ages, and the names of their authors lost. It is surely obvious that at all periods a writer may belong to more than one milieu. Third, Roberts plays down the role of Dyfed's govern-ment. 'Throughout the Four Branches the priority of Gwynedd is emphasized.' True; but we still hear repeat-edly of government in Dyfed, as with Pwyll meeting his leading men at Preseli, where they show themselves loyal but insistent. We may note that Pwyll successfully puts off their demands for a year, and that the author perhaps located the encounter near Crymmach, possibly at Foeldrygarn hillfort (SN 1533), by the main road south from Cardigan, which would be an apt place for an assem-bly of north and south Dyfed, and would show the author's knowledge of Dyfed's topography. Fourth, Roberts plays down the sustained emphasis in the *Four Branches* on Dyfed's territorial aggrandizement, which is again a theme hard to explain in a text of purely Gwynedd origin. Why should any writer in Gwynedd care about Dyfed's conquest of territories on its eastern frontier, so that by the fourth branch it has even absorbed Glamor-gan?

Fifth, Roberts is shaky on place names. It is true the author of the *Four Branches* was far more familiar with the geography of Gwynedd than that of Dyfed. Yet the knowl-edge displayed of Dyfed can still be shown as detailed and exact. Gorsedd Arberth is the prominent mound of Banc-y-Warren, two miles east of Cardigan; nearby Nant Arberth is still marked on Ordnance Survey maps; the Cuch runs along the Pembrokeshire-Carmarthenshire border; even Penn Llwyn Diarwya (hitherto unlocated) seems to be the fort (SN 2443) above modern Llwynduris (apparently preserving its name), where a hunter coming from near Cardigan to hunt by the Cuch might conveniently pass the night. Other spots might be mentioned, such as bleak and lonely Mochdref or Nant-y-môch (SN 7687), high up on the slopes of Pumlumon. The writer no doubt had a knowledge of Dyfed's geography that was limited, but could on occasion be precise. How can all these phenomena be accounted for by a hypothetical writer in Gwynedd, above all one in Clynnog? Why should any writer there acquire or wish to acquire such precise information on the topography of the lower Teifi or its environs?

If we are to escape from this quandary, we must rid ourselves of the either/or fallacy, of the assumption that the texts must be either Gwynedd ones or Dyfed ones, but not both. Every detail of the texts can without exception be explained if we seek an author who had a strong feeling for the landscape of Gwynedd, and an insider knowledge of its government, politics, and law, but who at the same time was committed to the cause of Dyfed. Readers will know the present writer proposes such an author in Gwenllian, daughter of Gruffudd ap Cynan, king of Gwynedd, and wife of Gruffydd ap Rhys, prince of Dyfed. As a Gwynedd princess married to a Dyfed prince, Gwenllian would have a natural allegiance to both realms. Hence (if she is our author) the dual loyalties of her stories. Hence the flattering words on both Dyfed ('they had never seen a land more delightful to live in, nor a better hunting ground, nor a land more abundant than that in honey and fish') and Dinoding ('the very best cantref for a young man to have'). Hence a commitment to the political advancement of both realms. (Dyfed's territorial advances are, significantly, not made against Gwynedd; nor does Dyfed lose territory to Gwynedd, even after military defeat.) Hence also the intimate knowledge the tales show of secular lordship, as also the striking absence from them of ecclesiastical learning or allusions to ecclesiastical sites.

As for Roberts's words on the literary tradition of Gwynedd, he speaks truer than he knows. If the view that Gwenllian composed these tales is correct, it explains parallels between them and *Historia Gruffudd ap Cynan;* which would be no surprise, since this is a life of her own father (and actually mentions her). The Irish aspects common to both the *Four Branches* and *Historia Gruffudd ap Cynan* have long been noted; but the descriptions of fighting near Clynnog (where Gruffudd lost the battle of Bron yr Erw in 1081) in both also seem more than coincidence.[7] Roberts further mentions the poetry of Hywel ab Owain Gwynedd. Here again there is a closer link than he knows. Owain was Gwenllian's own nephew, and it can be shown point by point that his poetry shares with the *Four Branches* items of vocabulary, which are rare or unknown elsewhere. If these texts are the work of nephew and aunt, no surprise: but if there is no such connection, these shared features are hard to explain.

III

The question of the dating, provenance, and authorship of the *Four Branches* thus seems to have a simple answer. Peculiarities of the text (the dual geography; the familiarity with government and politics in both Gwynedd and Dyfed) can be accounted for if we admit that the author was brought up in the Gwynedd royal family, but entered that of Dyfed. Even the emphasis on Gwynedd rather than Dyfed is explicable. Gruffudd ap Cynan was (in the end) a powerful ruler, but Gruffydd ap Rhys less so, with much of his ancestral land lost to the Normans. The hypothesis of a Gwynedd author moving in adult life to Dyfed also explains the intimate knowledge of Gwynedd, of scenes known from childhood in Anglesey and Caernarfon, as well as in the Bangor, Clynnog, Ffestiniog, and Trawsfynydd regions. Knowledge of Dyfed topography, coming in adult life, might on occasion be precise, but would naturally tend to be more limited (though experience of hunting would broaden it).

It is submitted, then, that the attribution to Gwenllian of the *Four Branches* resolves the question of their origin and date. If so, as regards when the *Four Branches* were written, the answer would be between about 1120, when Gwenllian had attained her majority (and married), and January 1136, when she was put to death at Kidwelly by the Anglo-Norman authorities. Some internal evidence points to a dating of 1128 or a little later. As to place of writing, the likely answer is Caio, eight miles south-east of Lampeter, where Gruffydd and Gwenllian spent their married life. Publication in this area would explain why these texts occur at an early date in southern manuscripts. Daniel Huws (formerly of the National Library of Wales) has linked the MS Peniarth 6 fragments with the Abbey of Strata Florida (SN 7465), which is sixteen miles north of Caio and was founded by the Lord Rhys, Gwenllian's son.[8] These manuscript fragments thus provide another clue as to why tales with a Gwynedd bias can be linked not merely with the south, but with the region around the Teifi, as also with the royal house of Dyfed.

Notes

1. B. F. Roberts, 'Where Were the Four Branches of the Mabinogi Written?', 61–75.
2. Cf. also Owen, 'Women's Place', 40–68; Wendy Davies, *Wales*, 211–12; Dark, *Civitas*, 229.
3. Lloyd-Morgan, 36–50.
4. Cf. Jackson, *International Popular Tale*, 129–30.
5. Cf. Sioned Davies, 7–8.
6. Jones and Jones, 60.
7. *Historia*, lxvii, cv, 68–9.
8. Huws, *Llyfrau Cymraeg*, 15, 19.

Ireland and the Tale of Branwen

The date of the Irish saga *Mesca Ulad* 'The Intoxication of the Ulstermen' has long been debated; so, too, has its importance as a source for the *Four Branches of the Mabinogi*. What follows thus investigates each subject, in the hope of shedding light on both.

I

Discussion effectively began here in the 1920s, with the work of Thurneysen and Cecile O'Rahilly. For *Mesca Ulad* the crucial date is 1921, when Thurneysen's *Heldensage* appeared; for the Welsh material it is 1924, when Cecile O'Rahilly in her *Ireland and Wales* set out the Irish analogues of the *Four Branches*. Thurneysen's conclusions were soon developed by Áine de Paor and summarized by Robin Flower. In the latter's words, a writer 'of the first quarter of the twelfth century' recast the somewhat crude compilation of *Táin Bó Cuailgne* in the 'bombastic, alliterative style which appears to have developed in the eleventh century and which became characteristic of the later literature. Thurneysen attributes to the same writer the second version of *Mesca Ulad* and the Book of Leinster version of *Cath Ruis na Ríg*'.[1]

In 1941 J. C. Watson accordingly quoted Thurneysen on the later version of *Mesca Ulad* as 'the work of the redactor of the Book of Leinster *Táin* (*Bearbeiter* C), and author of

Cath Ruis na Ríg'. Watson further described *Mesca Ulad* as written later than the *Táin*, which influenced its style. He thought *Mesca Ulad* much closer in style to the Book of Leinster *Táin* than either is to *Cath Ruis na Ríg*, which he took as the last of these works to be written.[2] However, T. F. O'Rahilly, a dissident voice, took issue with Thurneysen and described his dating for the Book of Leinster *Táin* as based on the flimsy evidence of the form of *Caladbolg* 'battle-gap', a sword of heroes.[3] Yet O'Rahilly's own views, though dogmatically expressed, found no followers. Commentators echoed Thurneysen. Walsh thus said of the Book of Leinster *Táin* that the redactor rewrote it, composed the tale of the battle of Ros na Riogh, and revised *Mesca Ulad*, his style becoming a model of Irish prose for five centuries; Dillon called him an unknown twelfth-century writer with a praiseworthy flowing style; Caerwyn Williams stated that in the first quarter of the twelfth century an editor known as 'C' put the *Táin* into bombastic form (a style developed in the eleventh century), uniting texts similar to those in the Books of the Dun Cow and Leinster, and adding material of his own.[4]

The watershed on this matter was in 1958, when Proinsias Mac Cana analyzed *Branwen*'s 'Irish affinities'. He discussed three obvious Irish borrowings here: the use of fire to try to destroy enemies trapped in an Iron House; the description of Bendigeidfran as a man-mountain; and an origin-legend of Ireland's five provinces. It is the first that concerns us here. Death in a blazing house is mentioned in the ninth- or tenth-century *Orgain Denna Ríg* 'The Destruction of Din Ríg', the Book of Leinster *Mesca Ulad*, usually dated to 1100–1125, and the tenth- or eleventh-century *Bórama* 'Cattle Tribute'. However, Mac Cana thought *Mesca Ulad* could not be *Branwen*'s source, since he dated that to the late eleventh or early twelfth century. He thus posited a lost earlier recension of *Mesca Ulad* containing the Iron House theme.[5]

Mac Cana's ideas were accepted by Jackson, who noted a Continental analogue of the Iron House theme in one of the Grimms' fairy tales, *Six Go Through the World*. Jackson thought the motif was perhaps of Continental origin (not Irish), and that more research might confirm this.[6] Yet the Iron House episode in *Branwen* can scarcely be treated independently of *Mesca Ulad*. So much was shown by Derick Thomson, who pointed out that *Branwen* is here much closer to *Mesca Ulad* than it is to other Irish texts. Since, however, he dated the Welsh tale to the second half of the eleventh century and the Book of Leinster *Mesca Ulad* to the twelfth, he had the same problem as Mac Cana. While Mac Cana posited a lost recension of *Mesca Ulad*, Thomas took the opposite tack, taking the passage in *Branwen* as a later interpolation.[7] It is argued below that both these conclusions are unfounded and there is thus no need to multiply entities.

Meanwhile, Thurneysen's views were still repeated. In editing the Book of Leinster *Táin*, Cecile O'Rahilly referred to Thurneysen's Bearbeiter C as one bringing the material of the *Táin* into a coherent whole. She also followed his dating of him (on his use of *s*-preterite and *f*-future, the *-it* ending of the third-person plural perfect passive, and the independent pronoun) to the first third or even first quarter of the twelfth century.[8]

In the 1970s consensus started to crack. It is true that Jarman in 1974 followed Mac Cana and Bromwich in viewing the Iron House motif as a deliberate literary borrowing in *Branwen* from Irish.[9] Yet the very opposite opinion was expressed only three years later, when Patrick Sims-Williams maintained that it was impossible to prove that *Branwen* borrows directly from Irish sources.[10] In 1981, Gearóid Mac Eoin challenged Thurneysen head on, describing his grounds for dating the Book of Leinster *Táin* as 'unusually flimsy', and noting the unfortunate effects this has had on later scholars, dazzled by Thurneysen's prestige and somewhat blindly following his path.[11] In 1986, Mac Gearailt published a detailed investigation of the language of these texts. At this point he did not deny Thurneysen's view that Bearbeiter C, active in the first quarter of the twelfth century, was effectively responsible for the three texts associated with him, though he noted the difficulties involved. Further, since he believed *Branwen* must predate 1100, he followed Mac Cana in deriving its Iron House incident from an earlier recension of *Mesca Ulad*, which he identified with his postulated text Q.[12] In 1987 Patrick Ford, like Sims-Williams, argued that no borrowing from Irish can be traced in *Branwen*.[13] That year Ó Concheanainn published his own analysis of *Mesca Ulad's* text, coming to the startling conclusion that the Book of Leinster version is probably the work of Áed Mac Crimthainn, the main compiler of this manuscript in about 1160; a view that well and truly overturns Thurneysen's apple cart.[14] Despite this, in 1990 Jackson still gave a date of the 'very early twelfth century' for Bearbeiter C.[15] It was clear the revisionists still had work to do.

Debate has continued since then. By the early 1990s Mac Gearailt had committed himself to the opinion that the Book of Leinster *Cath Ruis na Ríg* was written in the middle or later twelfth century by Áed Mac Crimthainn (the main scribe of this manuscript) or someone close to him, who was also responsible for the latter half of the Book of Leinster *Táin*, but was certainly not the author of *Mesca Ulad* in this manuscript, though he may have been influenced by its style.[16] This view, which goes against that of Ó Concheanainn, is presented with detailed analysis and is not easily dismissed. It will be obvious that, if correct, it has profound implications for the Irish elements in *Branwen*, where in this very period the court still showed itself out. In 1991 Patrick Sims-Williams declared that 'the date of the *Four Branches* is still very much an open question'; in 1992 Mac Cana, repudiating some of his earlier work, agreed; in 1995, when Professor Sioned Davies published a book-length study of the *Mabinogion*, she dated the *Four Branches* to between about 1050 and 1190.[17] In 1999, Professor Pádraig Ó Néill of North Carolina, citing Jackson, thought that Bearbeiter C 'the original author of the Book of Leinster *Táin*' could still be dated to the early twelfth century.[18]

II

How do we sum up the above debate, when there is still such disagreement amongst Irish scholars? Let us set down various opinions again and see if they can be reconciled. First, Mac Gearailt. In 1986 he followed Thurneysen in dating the Book of Leinster *Mesca Ulad* to 'the first quarter of the twelfth century'. In 1991 he stated as 'most unlikely' Thurneysen's thesis that the author of *Cath Ruis na Ríg* was also responsible for the Book of Leinster *Táin* and *Mesca Ulad*. He attributed *Cath Ruis na Ríg* to Áed mac Crimthainn or a young associate of Laois origin, active in the middle or later twelfth century. In 1992 he called Áed the 'author' of *Cath Ruis na Ríg*. In 1994 he referred to strong resemblances in language and style between the second half of the Book of Leinster *Táin* and *Cath Ruis na Ríg*.[19] All this seems to leave *Mesca Ulad* at the beginning of the century.

In flat contradiction is Ó Concheanainn, who attributes the Book of Leinster *Mesca Ulad* to Bearbeiter C, whom he takes as Áed Mac Crimthainn, the scribe-compiler of the Book of Leinster in about 1160.[20] Agreeing with neither are the shade of Jackson and Ó Néill, who follow Thurneysen in dating Bearbeiter C 'the original author of the Book of Leinster *Táin*' to the early twelfth century.[21]

Let us slice through this Irish knot. It is clear that those who attribute *Cath Ruis na Ríg* and the Book of Leinster *Táin* and *Mesca Ulad* to the same hand, whether writing in the early twelfth century or shortly before 1160, are on the defensive. As regards Welsh, what matters for present purposes is that the Book of Leinster *Mesca Ulad* with its iron house episode (a text nobody has dated before 1100) should be no later than about 1125 or so. That would allow time for it to become known to the author of the *Four Branches* by the late 1120s. Since no evidence has been brought forward to prove *Mesca Ulad* must postdate (say) 1130, its traditional dating to the very early twelfth century may be allowed to stand. If this shatters the concomitant view that the Book of Leinster *Mesca Ulad* and

Táin together with *Cath Ruis na Ríg* are the work of one writer/redactor, then so be it. In short, the second branch's apparent debt to *Mesca Ulad* for the iron house motif strengthens the case of those who, like Mac Gearailt, attribute the three Irish tales to two or more writers working at different dates. On this it seems Welsh studies and Irish studies may for once shake hands.

Notes

1. Thurneysen, *Die irische Helden- und Königsage*, 364, 473; Aine de Paor, 'Common Authorship', 118–46; Cecile O'Rahilly, *Ireland and Wales*, 106–12; Robin Flower, *Catalogue*, 294, 332.
2. *Mesca Ulad*, xix-xxv.
3. O'Rahilly, *Early Irish History and Mythology*, 68–72.
4. Walsh, *Irish Men of Learning*, 228; Dillon, *Early Irish Literature*, 3–4; J. E. C. Williams, *Traddodiad*, 91.
5. Mac Cana, *Branwen*, 16–23.
6. Jackson, *International Popular Tale*, 100–1.
7. *Branwen*, x-xi, xxxvi-xl.
8. *Táin Bó Cúalgne*, xlvi, liv.
9. Jarman, *'Pedair Cainc y Mabinogi'*, at 124–5.
10. Patrick Sims-Williams, 'Riddling Treatment', 83–117.
11. Mac Eoin, 'Dating of Middle Irish Texts', at 117.
12. Mac Gearailt, 'Edinburgh Text', 149–50 and 156.
13. Ford, *'Branwen'*, 29–41.
14. Ó Concheanainn, 'Manuscript', 13–30.
15. *Aislinge*, xxi.
16. Mac Gearailt, *'Cath Ruis na Ríg'*, 149, 'Language' 168, 191–2, and 'Relationship', 64.
17. Sims-Williams, 'Submission', 31–61; Mac Cana, *Mabinogi*, 2nd edn, 23, 132–3; Sioned Davies, *Crefft*, 8.
18. Ó Néill, 'Latin Colophon', 270.
19. Mac Gearailt, 'Edinburgh Text', 155–6. *'Cath Ruis na Ríg'*, 149, 'Language', 203, and 'Relationship', 64.
20. Ó Concheanainn, 'Manuscript', 19, 30.
21. Ó Néill, 'Latin Colophon', 270.

Topography and the *Four Branches*

Almost nine centuries after they were written, the *Four Branches* have more readers than ever. Minute critical analysis, together with translation into unfamiliar languages, alike pay tribute to their excellence.[1] Yet their date and place of composition are still problematic. On the second of these Brynley Roberts now proposes Clynnog Fawr (SH 4149), south of Caernarfon, calling it 'a strong candidate on both cultural and geographical grounds', and Patrick Sims-Williams agrees, thinking the tales show the influence of Clynnog's early religious community.[2] Whether this really holds water is considered at end of this chapter. Most of what follows, however, deals with the whereabouts of each place mentioned in the *Four Branches*. An attempt to locate exactly every toponym in these narratives will tell us much about their author's geographical knowledge, thereby sharpening our focus on these remarkable tales and whoever wrote them. Once that is done, we can look again at recent claims on where the *Four Branches* were written.

I

There are seventy-nine toponyms in the *Four Branches*, all but eight of them in Wales. In the first branch are ten; in the second, twenty-six; in the third, four, in the fourth, forty. This chapter deals with them as they appear, providing each where possible with a British national grid reference, locating them to within one square kilometre. Beside these are three and possibly four 'hidden' toponyms (one in Ireland, the others in Wales) which are not mentioned by name but which may be inferred from episodes in the stories.

The tale of Pwyll, Prince of Dyfed, contains ten place names: Arberth, Ceredigion, Dyfed, Glyn Cuch, Gorsedd Arberth, Gwent Is Coed, Penn Llwyn Diarwya, Preseli, Seissyllwch, and Ystrad Tywi. These are straightforward. All but one are in south-west Wales. Arberth is now recognized not as the large village of Narberth (SN 1014) in south Pembrokeshire, but as the farm of Arberth (SN 2046) a mile east of Cardigan, not far from the stream of Nant Arberth marked on modern Ordnance Survey maps.[3] The ancient kingdom of Ceredigion had almost the same bounds as the modern county of Ceredigion.[4] But the Dyfed of the *Four Branches* is smaller than the county of Dyfed created in 1974 and dissolved in 1996, as also the ancient territory occupied by the Demetae of Ptolemy. It effectively covered merely Pembrokeshire and west Carmarthenshire.[5] Glyn Cuch (SN 2539), where Pwyll meets the king of the Other World, is the valley of the river Cuch, running six miles north-west into the Teifi, and forming the boundary of Pembrokeshire and Carmarthenshire. Gorsedd Arberth (SN 2047), the mound of Arberth, is the conspicuous tumulus of Banc-y-Warren a mile east of Cardigan, by the main road to Aberystwyth, with supposed supernatural powers mentioned in the ninth-century *Historia Brittonum*.[6] Gwent Is Coed 'Gwent Below Wood' is the part of southern Monmouthshire between the rivers Wye and Ebbw.[7] The location of Penn Llwyn Diarwya 'hill of the grove of Diarwya' has been obscure. But it clearly lay between Arberth and Glyn Cuch, and was nearer the latter. Llwyn Diarwya may thus have been the modern hamlet of Llwynduris (SN 2434) by the` river Teifi, the *penn* being the hill with an ancient earthwork just east of it, a mile from where the Cuch joins the Teifi. Preseli, where Pwyll and his leading men took counsel, is the hill-range of Preseli (SN 0832) in north Pembrokeshire.[8] The author perhaps set the meeting at Foel Drygarn (SN 1533), an Iron Age fort 1200 feet up and a mile west of Crymych on the road south from Cardigan. This spot is equally accessible from north and south Dyfed, and would thus be a suitable place for a prince of Dyfed to consult with his barons about his successor.[9] Seissyllwch was an area comprising Ceredigion, Carmarthenshire east of Carmarthen, and the Gower Peninsula. It hence stretched from north of Aberystwyth down to Swansea, taking its name from Seisyll, the king of Ceredigion who (according to tradition) expanded his kingdom southwards in about the year 730, though it has been noted that early evidence for this is lacking.[10] Ystrad Tywi (SN 7861–SN 3610) was the southern part of that region, extending from the river Teifi southwards to the Gower Peninsula by modern Swansea.[11]

Two things may be inferred from the above. The author had an intimate knowledge of the lower Teifi valley, including even the minor stronghold above Llwyndyrys and Aber-cuch, if this is correctly identified as Penn Llwyn Diarwya. The author also had a strong belief in the military and political destiny of Dyfed, which has expanded by the end of the tale to cover all south-west Wales. Even Gwent Is Coed (the only place in the first branch that lies outside south-west Wales) is part of Dyfed's dominions, since Teyrnon, its lord, is described having been a vassal of Pwyll.

II

Many of the toponyms in the second branch, the tale of Branwen, are in north-west Wales. There are twenty-six of them: Aber Alaw, Aber Henfelen, Aberffraw, Abermenei, Archan, Ardudwy, Cernyw, Edeirnon, Ffreinc, Glan Alaw, Gwales, Gwynfryn, Harddlech, Iwerddon, Kaer Seint yn Arfon, Kymru, Lli, Llinon, Llundain, Llyn y Peir, Penfro, Seith Marchog, Talebolion, and Ynys y Kedeirn.

The Alaw is a river in west Anglesey; Aber Alaw (SH 3182) is its estuary, three miles east of Holyhead. Aber Henfelen is probably the Bristol Channel. At Aberffraw (SH 3568), now a sleepy village in south Anglesey, the princes of North Wales held court.[12] Abermenei (SH 4461) is in Anglesey, at the western mouth of the Menai Straits separating the island from the mainland.[13] Archan is a legendary river, which overflowed to make the Irish Sea. This hydronym, not recorded elsewhere, may be an error for *Arthan* 'bear cub', which is known as a personal name; there is also a river Arth 'bear' (SN 4763) in Ceredigion.[14] The author avoids references to places that do not exist, preferring to locate the narrative at sites (archaeological and other) which can be seen, as did Thomas Hardy in his Wessex novels. So this allusion to the Archan may well be a non-authorial gloss. Ardudwy is the rugged mountainous district by the north-east shore of Cardigan Bay, extending some twenty miles from the river Glaslyn south of Snowdon to the river Mawddach. It includes Harlech and Trawsfynydd.[15] Cernyw is Cornwall. Edeirnon or Edeirnion, a region where Bendigeidfran leaves a garrison for the defence of Britain (or rather Gwynedd) while he is in Ireland, lies on the middle part of the river Dee around Corwen (SJ 0743); it is the eastern part of Penllyn.[16]

Ffreinc is France. Glan Alaw (SH 3685) 'bank of Alaw' is a farm in north-west Anglesey; the tumulus where Branwen is buried is marked on the map as 'Bedd Branwen' (SH 3684). It was excavated in 1813 and the 1960s, revealing Bronze Age cremations with urns, beads of jet and amber, and a bone knife-pommel.[17] It is not likely that the *Four Branches* use an early tradition for this episode. The locating of a heroine's grave at this remote mound instead indicates the author's powerful creative imagination, peopling a landscape of ancient remains with the homes of the living and the tombs of the dead. Gwales, where Bendigeidfran's companions spent eighty joyous years, is the uninhabited island of Grassholm (SM 5909), about four hundred yards long, at the southern approaches to St Bride's Bay, twelve miles west of the Pembrokeshire mainland.

Gwynfryn, the 'white hill' in London, where Bendigeidfran's severed head was buried to ward off danger from France, is mysterious. Tower Hill is usually suggested, though Sir Ifor Williams preferred Ludgate Hill, where St Paul's Cathedral stands.[18] The first suggestion is preferable. Tower Hill faces towards the Continent; is associated with defence; and had links with France through the building of the Tower of London (known as being in progress in 1097), so that it would be familiar in twelfth-century Wales.[19] It was thus a far better place to bury an apotropaic head than Ludgate Hill is. Even now it is the home of apotropaic ravens, which allegedly ward off foreign invasion. Yet the name can have nothing to do with the White Tower there, since (a) a white tower is not the same as a white hill and (b) the great keep was not whitewashed until the thirteenth century.[20] Harddlech 'fair rock' is Harlech (SH 5831) in south Gwynedd, on a crag crowned by Edward I's fortress of 1283–9. There is no historical or archaeological evidence for a royal castle there of the native Welsh princes.[21] Yet the consistence references in the *Four Branches* to events located at ancient walls and earthworks may imply that there were defences at Harlech (perhaps prehistoric) which were destroyed when Edward I's castle was built.

Iwerddon is Ireland. Caer Seint yn Arfon is Caernarfon (SH 4762), Gwynedd. Its history is of interest. A mile east of the modern town is the Roman fort of Segontium, by the river Seint. This is the *caer* or fortress where Bendigeidfran held court, and where the starling sent by Branwen in Ireland settled on his shoulder and revealed the letter she had sent him.[22] Although Hugh of Avranches, Earl of Chester, had in about 1090 established a motte-and-bailey fort down by the sea (on a site where Edward I was to build his castle), his fort was in Welsh hands by 1115.[23] Kymru is Wales. The Lli is another legendary river (otherwise recorded only by the fourteenth-century bard Rhys Goch Eryri), which overflowed to create the Irish Sea. Its name is related to Welsh *llif* 'stream, flood'.[24] Llinon is now agreed not to be the river Shannon but the Liffey, at Dublin.[25] Llundein is London. The Welsh phrase meaning 'exalted with the crown of London' deserves comment. Henry I was crowned at Westminster (on 5 August 1100), as English kings had been ever since Harold in the January of 1066. The author of the *Four Branches* has therefore made an ancient Celtic tradition out of a custom less than a century old. Llyn y Peir means 'cauldron lake'. It seems futile to try and find it on maps of Ireland, though it was presumably near Dublin.[26] Penfro, which the island of Gwales was administratively part of, is the southernmost peninsula (with Pembroke in it) of modern Pembrokeshire.[27] (The author was here slightly inaccurate. Gwales or Grassholm is actually nearer the district of Rhos, north of Penfro.) Seith Marchog is Bryn Seith Marchog (SJ 0750), near Corwen in north-east Wales, and may be evidence for Bendigeidfran's original links with this area.[28] Talebolion 'end of the ridges' or 'end of the chasms' is north-west Anglesey.[29] Ynys y Kedeirn 'isle of the mighty' is Britain. The expression is unknown elsewhere.

Of these twenty-six toponyms, thirteen refer to Wales or places in Wales. Of those, eight are in north-west Wales. To them may be added a 'hidden' toponym. The mention of hurdles thrown down on Bendigeidfran's giant body (so that his troops may cross the Liffey) surely alludes to Baile Átha Cliath 'settlement of the ford of the hurdles', the Irish name of Dublin, and is further evidence for the author's absorbing interest in place-name lore.[30]

III

In the third branch, the tale of Manawydan, there are twelve toponyms (with a 'hidden' thirteenth). Seven of these have been met with before: Arberth, Dyfed, Ffreinc or France, Gorsedd Arberth, the Gwynfryn or White Hill, Llundein or London, and Ynys y Kedeirn. The other four are easily identified. Caint, where the invading Caswallon is gaining power, is the county of Kent. Henffordd, where Manawydan and his companions make a living as saddlers, is Hereford (SO 5040), on the Welsh border. Lloegr is England. Rhydychen, where homage is done to Caswallon, is Oxford (SP 5305), an increasing centre of English royal power in the second quarter of the twelfth century. Three other cities where Manawydan worked (as maker of shields and then shoes) are mentioned but not named. The last is said to be in England and perhaps the other ones are too. Even the vagueness of this says something of the author's psychology. The tales show an intimate and loving knowledge of the topography of south-west and north-west Wales. England's geography, in contrast, is somewhat hazy. But there can be no doubt as to its sinister aspect. England is associated with underhand commercial rivalry, foreign usurpation, and threatening military power. Great territories in the Isle of the Mighty have been wrested from the Welsh. What remains to them, the much-loved territory of Wales, is also under threat. The mental ethos of this may perhaps suit the reign of Henry I, when Wales was forcibly constrained by his power.

Of the twelve place names, then, three (Arberth, Dyfed, and Gorsedd Arberth) are in south-west Wales, the others all beyond Wales. As for the thirteenth 'hidden' toponym, this is Caer Gawg 'bowl fort', which seems alluded to by the mysterious fort where Pryderi and Rhiannon are trapped by a golden bowl. This clearly lay near Arberth; but Sir Ifor Williams related it to Caer Gawch, home of the father of St Non, the mother of St David. This again may have been the Roman fort at Pumsaint (SN 6540), detected under the village cricket pitch, near the Roman gold mines at Dolau Cothi in north-east Carmarthenshire.[31] If Ifor Williams was right in seeing a connection, the author may have transferred a toponym from Carmarthenshire to Ceredigion, complete with the detail of the beautiful but dangerous golden bowl.

IV

The fourth branch, the tale of Math son of Mathonwy, is full of toponyms. There are forty-two, plus two allusions to places not directly named. Aber Menei and Ardudwy have already been mentioned. Arfon 'opposite Môn, opposite Anglesey' is the district in Gwynedd west of Bangor, containing most of Snowdonia.[32] It abutted Arllechwedd, the mountainous region extending east of it to the river Conway.[33] Arwystli is in central Wales, the south-west part of the former Montgomeryshire; one of its ancient centres of government was Caersws (SO 0391).[34] Bryn Arien was taken by Ifor Williams as Trwyn Maen Dylan (SH 4252), a headland on the coast seven miles south of Caernarfon.[35] Bryn Cyfergyr is now Bryn Cyfergyd (SH 722413), east of Ffestiniog.[36] Caer Aranrhod (SH 4254) is a rock exposed at low tide half a mile off the coast of Gwynedd.[37] The location of Caer Dathyl yn Arfon has been difficult, though Ifor Williams thought it might be near Caernarfon; it may have been the Twthill (SH 6348), a small rugged hill (with an ancient rock-cut ditch by its summit) in the north of Caernarfon town.[38] Cefyn Clun Tyno is a hill located by Ifor Williams near the farm of Coetyno (SH 4350), below Bron yr Erw, near Clynnog. In 1075 a battle was fought near it by Gruffudd ap Cynan.[39] Ceredigion has been noted. Ceri was south-eastern Montgomeryshire, around the village of Ceri (SO 1490).[40] Ceuwyrion is the modern farm of Cororion (SH 5968), three miles south of Bangor. Afon Gynfael is the river Cynfal (SH 7241), flowing westwards into the Vale of Ffestiniog.

Deheubarth 'southern part', originally all South Wales, was from the later tenth century used of the region of Dyfed, Ceredigion, and Ystrad Tywi, with its capital at Dinefwr (SN 6121), Carmarthenshire.[41] Dinas Dinlleu (SH 4356) is a hillfort, now being eroded by the sea, four miles south-west of Caernarfon.[42] Dinoding is a region consisting of Eifionydd and Ardudwy, around the north-east corner of Cardigan Bay.[43] Dôl Benmaen 'meadow of the rocky headland' is Dolbenmaen (SH 5043), on the road south of Caernarfon. Dôl Pebin is a farm near Nantlle (SH 5053), by hills now disfigured with slate quarries. Dyfed has been mentioned. Eifynyd is Eifionydd, the region on the north shore of Cardigan Bay, with its capital at Criccieth (SH 5038), near its western limit, though its original *caput* may have been at Dolbenmaen, where a defensive mound can still be seen.[44] Elenid is Elennydd, the old name of the massif separating Ceredigion from Powys, where the river Elan (SN 8374) and other major Welsh rivers have their source.[45] Y Felenrhyd is now Felenrhyd (SH 6439) 'mill ford'.[46] Gwynedd is the old realm and modern county of north-west Wales. Its heartland consisted of Anglesey, Arfon, Arllechwedd, Lleyn, Eifionydd, and Ardudwy.[47]

Llech Gronwy is now Llech Gronw (SH 716406), a pierced slab still existing in a wood near Ffestiniog, where it was rediscovered in January 1990. It is just over five foot long and nearly three feet wide, with its hole five inches across.[48] Another 'hidden' toponym is Llyn y Morynion (SH 7342) 'lake of maidens', east of Ffestiniog, where Blodeuedd's maids drowned as they fled eastwards, looking back for pursuers (the actual name and the explanation of it having been accidentally dropped from the text); it has been proposed they were making for the stronghold of Bryn y Castell (SH 7443), an iron age settlement now excavated and open to the public.[49] If so, this would be yet another ancient site known to the author. Maenawr Bennardd is the region around the farm of Pennarth, between Clynnog (SH 4149) and Llanllyfni (SH 4751); Maenawr Coed Alun 'manor of the wood of Alun' is now represented by Coed Helen (SH 4762), a hill facing Caernarfon Castle. The battle was fought on the meeting place of these areas.[50] Maen Tyriog, where Pryderi is buried, is Maentwrog (SH 6640). Mochnant 'pig stream' is in Llanrhaeadr-ym-Mochnant (SJ 1226), on the modern Powys-Denbighshire border. Mochdref 'pig farm' is represented by Nant-y-Moch (SN 7687), high up on the slopes of Pumlumon; the other Mochdref, in Rhos, is now

Mochdre (SH 8278), near Colwyn Bay. Morgannwg is effectively the modern Glamorgan (minus the Swansea and Gower regions) and Monmouthshire.[51] Mur Castell 'castle wall', where Blodeuedd entertained her lover, is Tomen y Mur (SH 7038) 'mound of the wall', a Roman camp (with an eleventh-century motte) overlooking Snowdonia.[52] Nant Call is now a farm near Pantglas (SH 4747) in the great pass between Arfon and Eifionydd. Nantlleu (SH 5053) has already been mentioned.[53] Penllyn is an area east of Ardudwy, with Bala Lake (SH 9032) at its heart.[54] The boundaries of Powys differed from those of the modern county, excluding what is now south Powys, but including a large area around Wrexham.[55]

Rhos in North Wales, between the rivers Conway and Clwyd, is approximately the modern county of Conwy.[56] Rhuddlan Teifi (SN 4349) is in south Ceredigion, above the river Teifi. The court where Pwyll entertained his visitors was at Pentre Rhuddlan, a little to the east, by the mansion of Highmead. The author's choice of this spot may have been influenced by Nant Creuddyn 'pigsty brook' (SN 5551) six miles east, which Gwydion would cross with the stolen swine on his escape northwards. If so, this shows the author using intimate knowledge of place-names to create a narrative (the toponym hardly derives from the tale), and can be added to our list of 'hidden' toponyms.[57] Y Traeth Mawr (SH 5939) 'the great beach' is the former estuary (drained in the early nineteenth century) south of Snowdonia, and separating Eifionydd and Ardudwy.[58] Ystrad Tywi has been mentioned above.

Another possible 'hidden' name is Rhyd y Pedestri 'ford of the foot-soldiers'. After their defeat near Caernarfon, Pryderi's army withdraws south under truce. But as soon as they reached Y Felenrhyd (SH 6439), 'the men on foot (*pedyt*) could not be restrained from shooting at each other'. W. J. Gruffydd connected this with Rhyd y Pedestri, a ford on Afon Foryd (SH 4457) in the marshes east of Dinas Dinlleu.[59] A difficulty here is that Afon Foryd is seventeen miles as the crow flies from Y Felenrhyd. Yet it may be that there was another unrecorded Rhyd y Pedestri near Y

Felenrhyd; or that the author has merged the two places.

Of the forty-two toponyms of the fourth branch, all are in north-west Wales except for Arwystli, Ceri, and Mochnant (Powys), and Elennydd, Mochdref, and Rhuddlan Teifi (Ceredigion), and the territorial forms Deheubarth, Dyfed, Ceredigion, Morgannwg, Powys, and Ystrad Tywi, which are in southern or eastern Wales.

V

What conclusions does the above lead to? There seem at least four. First is the overwhelming emphasis on the topography of north-west and south-west Wales. This has of course always been known, but the pinpointing of minor sites brings home the author's close knowledge of the topography of Gwynedd and Ceredigion. Second is the creative way in which real places and toponyms are used. Especially striking is how many places here (Gorsedd Arberth, Bedd Branwen, Mur Castell, and perhaps Penn Llwyn Diarwya and the assembly place on Preseli) are archaeological ones. Histories of archaeology of Wales usually ignore the *Four Branches* or deal with them in a perfunctory way.[60] Yet they deserve special mention for their sustained response to Wales's past. It is possible that this unusual familiarity with certain parts of Wales was due to experience of hunting, as well as contact with royal administration. Third is the negative and threatening impression the narratives give of England. Although Bendigeidfran is called crowned king of Britain, he is effectively king of Gwynedd alone. Little is said of territory beyond Wales and what is said is linked with foreign invasion and national defeat. The political and ideological implications of this, with the tales showing Welsh consciousness of lost territory and sovereignty, are evident.

Fourthly, what do the seventy-nine toponyms in the text indicate as regards its provenance? Here we may deal especially with recent descriptions of it as the work of the religious community at Clynnog. This has two grave defects. There is nothing to show that the tales are the work of clerics; and there is nothing to show they were composed at Clynnog. (Elsewhere in this book we have set out arguments deriving from close analysis of the narrative that point to lay authorship.) Evidence for scriptural or other ecclesiastical learning, and for attention to church lands, are equally absent. As for Clynnog itself, which is not actually mentioned anywhere in the stories, this is quickly dealt with. True, the *Four Branches* show intimate knowledge of the Clynnog area, or more precisely of the road going due south from Caernarfon to the Portmadoc area and then east into the Vale of Ffestiniog. But they show also unusual knowledge of the lower Teifi valley. Here may be mentioned Pwyll's hunting-ground by the river Cuch, the mound of Arberth, the Preseli mountains as a place of regional assembly, Llwynduris (if we are correct in taking Penn Llwyn Diarwya as the hillfort by it), and Rhuddlan Teifi (especially if nearby Nant Creuddyn explains the choice of it as Pryderi's court). Why should clerics at a religious community in Lleyn know or care for the geography of the Teifi valley? Still more, why should they or their audience have such interest in the political advancement of Dyfed, so that by the close of the fourth branch it has swallowed up much of South Wales? Another and very different explanation of these phenomena seems more compelling.

The sites near Clynnog are not mentioned in a religious or ecclesiastical context, but a military or political one. The northern army awaits attack 'in the fastness of Gwynedd in Arfon', making a stand in the midmost part of Maenawr Bennardd and Maenawr Coed Alun. Presumably this was along the ridgeline north-east of Bwlch Fawr, where the old road north (now a mere lane) reaches its highest point before descending to cross the river Llyfni at Pont-y-Cim (SH 4452), two miles west of the present-day A 4085 trunk road between Portmadoc and Caernarfon. The summit of this wide mountain pass would be the spot to block any attack from the south. Certainly the places to which the southern forces retreat 'after great slaughter' (the author is careful to state that the men of the South fight bravely) are on the return route: Nant Call, Dôl Benmaen, Y Traeth Mawr, Maen Tyriawg. Later, Cefyn Clun Tyno is mentioned as the place where Gwydion and Lleu make towards Caer Aranrhod. Although they have started from Dinas Lleu to the north of Caer Aranrhod, they have to pass it and return from the south, crossing the Llyfni at Pont-y-Cim, since they are pretending to be bards from Glamorgan.

It is reasonable to conclude that the author shows interest not in Clynnog, but in the use of the old north-south route via Pont-y-Cim for military action and for intrigue. For the first there was a precedent well known at the court of Gwynedd in the early twelfth century. It was on terrain north-east of Bwlch Fawr (SH 6247) that Gruffudd ap Cynan lost the battle of Bron yr Erw in 1075, after which he retreated north towards Abermenai along the very road that Math and his troops took southwards against Pryderi (a fact noted by Ifor Williams). Gwydion and Lleu also travel on this road in their bid to outwit Aranrhod. The author of the *Four Branches* must have known this. The location of the bloody battle between the forces of Math and Pryderi is hence surely based on memories of Gruffudd ap Cynan's campaign at the same location. The inplications of this are dealt with elsewhere in this book. But they leave no room for the possibility that the *Four Branches* are the work of a cleric at Clynnog Fawr, in Lleyn.

Notes
1. Sioned Davies, *Crefft*; Erlikhman, *Mabinogion*.
2. Roberts, 'Where Were the *Four Branches of the Mabinogi* Written?', 61–75; Sims-Williams, 'Clas Beuno', 111–27; Russell, 'Texts', 59–72.
3. Gruffydd, *Rhiannon*, 18 n. 1; *Pwyll*, 24.
4. Lloyd, *History*, 256–60; Rees, *Historical Atlas*, plate 22.
5. Lloyd, *History*, 261–6; Rees, *Historical Atlas*, plate 22; Rivet and

Smith, *Place-Names*, 333.

6. Lloyd, *History*, 260, 473.
7 Lloyd, *History*, 278; Rees, *Historical Atlas*, plate 28.
8. Lloyd, *History*, 263.
9. Houlder, *Wales*, 180.
10. Lloyd, *History*, 257; Rees, *Historical Atlas*, plate 22; Wendy Davies, *Wales*, 110.
11. Lloyd, *History*, 266–9; Rees, *Historical Atlas*, plate 28.
12. Lloyd, *History*, 231, 682; Rees, *Historical Atlas*, plate 28; White, 'New Light', 350–5; Wendy Davies, *Wales*, 97.
13. *Historia*, 60.
14. Lloyd-Jones, *Geirfa*, 43; R. J. Thomas, *Enwau*, 187.
15. Lloyd, *History*, 238; Rees, *Historical Atlas*, plate 28.
16. Lloyd, *History*, 245; Rees, *Historical Atlas*, plate 28.
17. Houlder, *Wales*, 38–40.
18. *Trioedd*, 92.
19. Brown, *History*, 29–32.
20. For information on the White Tower I thank Professor Richard Coates.
21. Taylor, *Harlech Castle*, 4.
22. Boon, *Segontium*; Houlder, *Wales*, 56–7.
23. Lloyd, *History*, 234–5; Taylor, *Caernarvon Castle*, 7–8; Loomis, *Wales*, 4–5.
24. *Geiriadur*, 2177; *Poems of Taliesin*, 63.
25. Sims-Williams, 'Submission', 38.
26. Mac Cana, *Branwen*, 38 n. 1.
27. Lloyd, *History*, 265; Rees, *Historical Atlas*, plate 28.
28. Mac Cana, *Branwen*, 135–7.
29. Rees, *Historical Atlas*, plate 28; Mac Cana, *Branwen*, 156–8.
30. Mac Cana, *Branwen*, 118.
31. *Pedeir Keinc*, 238; *Welsh Life*, 27.
32. Lloyd, *History*, 233; Rees, *Historical Atlas*, plate 28.
33. Lloyd, *History*, 235–6; Rees, *Historical Atlas*, plate 28.
34. Lloyd, *History*, 249–50; Rees, *Historical Atlas*, plate 28.
35. *Pedeir Keinc*, 278–9.
36. *Pedeir Keinc*, 289.
37. *Trioedd*, 278.
38. *Pedeir Keinc*, 251–2; Taylor, *Caernarvon Castle*, 5.
39. *Pedeir Keinc*, 280; *Historia*, 68–9.
40. Lloyd, *History*, 253; Rees, *Historical Atlas*, plate 28.
41. Lloyd, *History*, 256, 267–8; Rees, *Historical Atlas*, plate 23.
42. *Trioedd*, 278.
43. Lloyd, *History*, 238; Rees, *Historical Atlas*, plate 28.
44. Lloyd, *History*, 238; Rees, *Historical Atlas*, plate 28.

45. R. J. Thomas, *Enwau*, 65–6.
46. *Pedeir Keinc*, 263.
47. Lloyd, *History*, 229–39; Rees, *Historical Atlas*, plates 28, 29.
48. G. V. Jones, 'Llech Gronw', 131–3.
49. *Pedeir Keinc*, 301.
50. *Pedeir Keinc*, 260–1, 262–3.
51. Lloyd, *History*, 275–8; Rees, *Historical Atlas*, plate 23; Wendy Davies, *Wales*, 103–4.
52. *Pedeir Keinc*, 285; Houlder, *Wales*, 103–4.
53. *Pedeir Keinc*, 291.
54. Lloyd, *History*, 245–6; Rees, *Historical Atlas*, plate 28.
55. Lloyd, *History*, 242–56; Rees, *Historical Atlas*, plate 28.
56. Lloyd, *History*, 239–40; Rees, *Historical Atlas*, plate 28.
57. Lloyd, *History*, 260; R. J. Thomas, *Enwau*, 87.
58. Lloyd, *History*, 238; R. J. Thomas, *Enwau*, 136.
59 Samuel Lewis, *Topographical Dictionary*, 541; W. J. Gruffydd, *Math*, 338–9.
60. Glyn Daniel, 'Introduction', 1–15.

St David, Caio, and the *Four Branches*

A tradition about St David has unexplored links with Welsh archaeology. David's mother was St Non, and her father was (according to an early genealogy) Cynyr of Caer Gawch. Nothing more is known of Cynyr, but in the 1920s A. W. Wade-Evans located Caer Gawch near Caio (SN 6742) in north-east Carmarthenshire. Caer Gawch was also associated by Sir Ifor Williams with a mysterious caer with a golden bowl (*cawg*) in the *Four Branches of the Mabinogi*: a magic fortress where Pryderi and Rhiannon are led into a trap.

A fort near Caio in Carmarthenshire is one thing. A fort of Celtic romance, containing treasure (but vanishing into mist and taking those inside with it), seems quite another. Yet this chapter proposes that more connects the two than one might think. Its examination of Caer Gawch thus falls into four parts. The first surveys previous discussion of St David and Cynyr; the second, Caio's history; the third, the 'fortress of the bowl' in the *Four Branches*; while the fourth examines how far all this material can be brought into a whole. If successful, it will help sharpen our focus on Welsh archaeology and tradition alike.

I

First, Cynyr and his fortress of Caer Gawch. Baring-Gould and Fisher provided a useful starting point here. They long ago described St Non as the daughter of Cynyr of Caer Gawch in Mynyw (the St Davids area), though they noted that David's biographers make no mention of Cynyr or Caer Gawch. Nor is there any trace of Caer Gawch near St Davids. Yet they felt sure *Cynyr* represented Irish *Conaire*, so that David would have had Irish blood via his mother. Such an Irish connection is no surprise, given the density of early Irish settlement in Dyfed (an area of many ogham inscriptions). Baring-Gould and Fisher nevertheless did not connect this Irish Cynyr with Cynyr 'Whitebeard' of Caio, Carmarthenshire, father of the confessors Gwyn, Gwyno, Gwynoro, Celynin, and Ceitho, whose shrine was at Pumsaint 'five saints'.[1]

Cynyr and Caer Gawch caught the attention of Sir John Lloyd, writing at the same time. Lloyd believed St Non really existed, about the year 520, thinking the cult of Non in Cornwall and Brittany (as well as Wales) otherwise inexplicable. Nevertheless, he dismissed references in *Bonedd y Saint* to her father Cynyr and to Caer Gawch as having 'no importance'. He also expressed scepticism on a connection between Sant (David's father) and the royal house of Ceredigion.[2]

In 1920 Ifor Williams associated Caer Gawch with the *Four Branches*, suggesting Cynyr's fort inspired the caer of the *cawg*, a golden bowl (suspended by chains above a marble slab) that lures Pryderi and Rhiannon into danger.[3] But the weightiest comment here was made by Wade-Evans. He noted that one manuscript of David's genealogy in *Bonedd y Saint* calls the spot 'Caer Gawc', and another omits 'in Mynyw'. He also cited references by Gerald of Wales to the commot of Caio as *Kaoc*, adding that Pumsaint in this commot appears in the Book of Llandaff as *pimpsaint kaircaiau*. He thus concluded that Caer Gawch, Caer Gawc, *Kaoc*, and *Kaircaiau* were one and the same place. He believed this possibility was strengthened by 'A Kalendar of Welsh Saints' in Aberystwyth, National Library of Wales, MS Cwrtmawr 44 (of the later sixteenth century). This describes the father of the 'five saints' (who were quintuplets) as Cynyr 'Whitebeard' of

Cynwyl Gaeo, Carmarthenshire.[4] Varied sources thus indicate Cynyr's links with the region of Caio, while there is nothing to prove that Caer Gawch was near St Davids.

Evidence from Scotland and Ireland reinforces Wade-Evans's arguments. Non's father Cynyr bore a name which surely represents Irish 'Conaire'. If *Cynyr* is not Welsh but Irish, the same might be true of the form giving *Cawch*. An Irish chieftain might give his Welsh fort an Irish name. If he did, we should find parallels elsewhere in Gaelic world; and it seems we do. Watson mentioned Scottish streams called Quaich or Queich, which he derived from *Cuach* 'cup, bowl'. He thought these streams were so called because they had many potholes.[5] Yet that is dubious. The most obvious of these streams is the River Quaich (NN 8039), flowing through a glacial valley east of Loch Tay. Most of Glen Quaich (partly occupied by Loch Freuchie) is flat, being filled with alluvial sediment. One would not seek potholes there. It has its name surely because the glen is a 'bowl' or 'hollow' in the mountains. This interpretation is supported by the remote crofting settlement of Cuaig (NG 7057), in a hollow near Applecross in Wester Ross; by Coagh (*An Cuach* 'The Hollow') in a shallow valley in Tyrone; and perhaps by Coa (H 2850) north of Enniskillen, Fermanagh. They would have a semantic parallel in the river Cib (from *cib* 'bowl') in a bowl-like valley south-east of Llandeilo, Carmarthenshire.[6]

Citing Wade-Evans's work (though hardly with Cynyr in mind), R. T. Jenkins made a comment that is pregnant in the present context. He emphasized Irish influence in Dyfed, declaring that the narrative accounts of David and the *Four Branches* 'live and move' in an Irish ambience, and that David himself was 'more of an Irishman than a Welshman'.[7] Despite mentioning Caer Gawch, Ifor Williams in his edition of the *Four Branches* unfortunately failed to pick up Wade-Evans's association of it with Caio, though it would have reinforced his arguments that the tales are by a Dyfed author.[8]

The next step was taken by John Lloyd-Jones (who

reviewed Wade-Evans's book in *Y Llenor* for 1923). He pointed out that *gwlat gynyr* and *tir kynyr* 'Cynyr's land' occur in poems by Madog Dwygreig, that *Tir Cynir* is mentioned in the twelfth-century Book of Llandaff, and that Cynyr is called St Non's father in a poem by Ieuan ap Rhydderch.[9] These references are significant. Madog Dwygreig (writing about 1370) addressed his poems to Morgan ap Dafydd ap Llywelyn, who lived at Rhydodyn or Edwinsford (SN 6334), four miles south-west of Caio. Morgan, of a family generous in its patronage of Welsh literature, was a famous benefactor of poets.[10] So in Madog's day the Caio district was still known as the land of Cynyr. The Book of Llandaff document is more problematic. It can be dated to about 900, but its *Tir Cynir* has been unlocated, though the grant itself is from a Gwent archive.[11] Yet the mysterious *Tir Cynir* may have been the commot of Caio, especially since Llandaff later claimed property at Llandeilo Garth Tefyr (SN 6537) and nearby Pumsaint, as we shall see below.

In his later study of Ceredigion, Sir John Lloyd noted how strong David's connections are with the south of the region, but how little evidence there is for him north of the river Aeron (where we enter the terrain of St Padarn).[12] Nora Chadwick also commented on David's links with Ceredigion, where his father Sant was king, and where he was educated and ordained. She thought Rhygyfarch in the late eleventh century was uneasy about placing David's conception and birth in Dyfed, far from Ceredigion.[13] She implied that older tradition located David's origins in south Ceredigion, and not near St Davids. This would accord with traditions that put St Non's family near Caio, just south of Ceredigion, but far from St Davids.

Recent comment may be summed up briefly. The genealogy mentioning Cynyr and Caer Gawch (compiled in the twelfth century) now appears in book form.[14] Bowen gave a useful list of shrines of St Non in Wales, Cornwall, and Brittany, though citing evidence from the last (noted by Canon Doble in the 1920s) that Non was a man.[15] Rachel Bromwich tends to associate Cynyr the father of Non with Cynyr 'the Fair-Bearded', father of King Arthur's Sir Kay.[16] But this cannot be so, as was made clear by the account of Baring-Gould and Fisher cited above. Non's father lived in south-west Wales; Kay's father in the region around Bala in North Wales, as is shown by the name of Caer-gai (SH 8731), another Roman fort. Non's cult in Cornwall is mentioned by Padel, who explains Altarnun (SW 2281) there as 'Non's altar', but Pelynt (SX 2055) as 'Nennyd's parish', perhaps the male saint confused with Non in later tradition.[17] Dumville also provides useful references to Non's cult and her appearance in medieval Breton drama, though he says nothing on her father Cynyr.[18]

The reference by Ieuan ap Rhydderch (*c.*1390–*c.*1470) to Non as Cynyr's daughter therefore deserves special attention. Two points may be made here. First, editors observe how the bards (including Iolo Goch in the fourteenth century) refer to Cynyr as Non's father, when nothing is said of this in the Latin and Welsh prose lives. Second, Ieuan's biography confirms what was said above about Madog Dwygreig. Ieuan was the son of Rhydderch ab Ieuan, of Parcrhydderch (SN 6058), some eleven miles north of Caio. Ieuan's father is famous as the patron of the White Book of Rhydderch, containing the oldest copy of the *Four Branches of the Mabinogi*.[19] So Ieuan came from a family of strong literary interests, who had long been settled in the Upper Teifi area. His allusion to St Non's father thus underlines Cynyr's persistent association with the Caio region: a subject of interest to local poets, and of no interest to writers in St Davids.

What does all this suggest? Although documents from St Davids might be expected to cherish David's ancestry, they ignore Cynyr. Nor does anything confirm the statement in *Bonedd y Saint* that Caer Gawch was near St Davids. The evidence suggests instead that Cynyr and his fort were located some sixty miles to the east, in the region of Caio. Even at the end of the middle ages we find poets there taking care to mention the name of Cynyr, grandfather of St David. If, then, we are to find Caer

Gawch, we should clearly look for it around Caio, and not St Davids.

II

That concludes the first part of this paper, on Cynyr and Caer Gawch. We now turn to Caio (in Welsh, *Cynwyl Gaeo*) and what historians and archaeologists say of it. There is a wealth of material. Still of interest are Samuel Lewis's remarks of the 1840s. He observed Caio appears to have been 'formerly of much greater importance than it is at present', an older name *Caer Caio* 'evidently implying that it was defended either by a castle or some other military work' (his acute observation was vindicated in 1972, as noted below). Lewis described in detail the Roman remains found there, including bricks; the remains of gold mines (with 'vestiges of a stupendous Roman aqueduct'); gold torques found locally and preserved at Dolau Cothi House; 3000 copper coins discovered in 1762, dated to the time of Gallienus (253–68) and the 'thirty tyrants'; and the tessellated pavements and hypocaust of a bathhouse excavated in 1831. Lewis also mentioned local early Christian monuments, giving the inscription (to Paulinus) of one of them.[20]

In the early twentieth century, Sir John Lloyd looked at Caio with the eye of a historian (not an archaeologist). He referred to the commot of Caio, in the upper reaches of the Cothi and at the heart of Cantref Mawr ('great cantref'), as a land 'where nature ever gave the sons of the soil her kindly, overshadowing protection' (i.e., it was fertile). He also noted Caio as the home of Gruffydd ap Rhys and his wife Gwenllian, daughter of Gruffudd ap Cynan, king of Gwynedd, and mother of the great Lord Rhys.[21]

Lloyd's perspective was not the normal one. Most twentieth-century writers on Caio dealt with its Roman remains. Here the gold mine, appearing routinely in accounts of Roman Britain, has first place. Collingwood thus referred to the remains at Dolau Cothi (SN 6640) a mile from Caio village, with an aqueduct supplying water for washing the ore, a bathhouse for the miners (it appears too large for a manager's private use), and abundant finds of jewellery worked by goldsmiths on the spot. He thought the mine must have been state property and was possibly under military control, 'though of this there is no evidence'.[22]

A. H. Williams, summarizing Lloyd's history, was unusual in bringing Roman remains and medieval records together. On the first he mentioned the seven-mile water-channel and the collection of jewellery and ornaments, 'probably the finest of its kind in these islands'.[23] In a survey of Roman Wales, Randall referred to the pavements of the pithead baths; the seven-mile water conduit, most of it cut out of solid rock (with gaps bridged presumably by wooden troughs on trestles); and the splendid hoard of gold objects found at the end of the eighteenth century and now in the British and Carmarthen Museums. He also makes the rash statement that 'there is not the slightest trace of a fort', that a gold mine was hence apparently worked with 'the very slightest amount of military protection', so that the Roman peace was 'indeed pervasive'.[24] Charlesworth observed that the Roman hoped to discover gold in Britain, but what little they found was mostly at Dolau Cothi. There is no clear indication that they knew of the gold resources in Merioneth.[25]

Caio's post-Roman monuments received attention from Nash-Williams. He edited its three inscriptions of this date, all of the sixth century. The first, in two barbarous hexameters, commemorates Paulinus, 'preserver of faith, constant lover of his country, devoted champion of righteousness'; the others commemorate Talorius, and Reginus son of Nudintus. The first may refer to Paulinus, teacher of St David and of Bishop Bivatigirnus whose wisdom was 'more precious than gold', and whose memorial still stands at Llantrisaint, Anglesey.[26] But this is not certain (as we shall see). However, all the Caio inscriptions were surely to persons of status.

Richmond discussed Caio briefly but with authority,

mentioning expert cutting of adit galleries for drainage and haulage, drainage by wheels to lift water, a bath-house resembling that at Aljustrel in Portugal, and jewellery dated to about AD 200. He described the scale of operations as showing 'high standing and efficiency'.[27] Frere added that the aqueduct would have supplied three million gallons of water daily, apparently to break down softer beds of rock as well as to wash the ore, that fire-setting was also used to penetrate the rock, and that the whole 'illustrates the most impressive aspects of Roman mining technology'. Significantly, he thought the bath-house at Pumsaint (SN 6540) was probably that of an unlo-cated fort.[28] Liversedge likewise described the technological processes of mining, as well as massive gold serpent armlets found near the mines.[29]

An important and original approach to Caio was given by Glanville Jones, who related its archaeological past to a grant ('Chad 4') of about 850 in the Book of St Chad, now at Lichfield. He cited the Paulinus inscription from Maes-llanwrthwl (SN 6537) as showing the privileged status of this region, though noting the difficulties of identifying him with St David's tutor of the sixth century, and argu-ments that take him rather as a secular ruler of the fifth. He gave a survey of Roman remains, including 682 radiates found in 1965 at Erw Hen, three miles north of Caio. The bathhouse he thought indicated a fort nearby, perhaps at Pumsaint. He observed that there must have been a large community of miners living here from the first century to the third (when the mines were worked), but that nothing is known of operations between the third century and the nineteenth. He cited a verse in the thirteenth-century Black Book of Carmarthen on 'a man who would not shun conflict', Dyfel son of Erbin, whose grave is in 'the plain of Caio', suggesting this indicates this region's post-Roman importance. He also referred to an annual tribute imposed in 926 by Athelstan on the Welsh which included three hundred pounds of silver and twenty pounds of gold. This he suggested might indicate mining at Caio in this period.

Finally, Jones cited the Book of Llandaff claim to

lannteliau pimseint caircaiau 'The church of St Teilo of the five saints of the fort of Caio'. This is our Pumsaint, and makes a clear reference to local fortification. Jones proposed a connection between Gwynio, one of these confessors, and Ffynnon Gwenno, a spring (inside the Roman workings) with supposed curative powers. He also linked the five saints with five hollows on a block of diorite (supposed to show the impression of their heads, but actually used to crush out gold from quartz) that the Romans imported to the locality. (But Jones did not cite a further legend of Gwynio mentioned by Baring-Gould and Fisher. Despite warnings, she ventured into a cave beyond a frowning rock and was no more seen alive, though her spirit hovers on stormy moonlit nights 'like a wreath of mist' over a nearby crag.) Jones interpreted the non-folkloric parts of the legend as indicating administrative continuity at Caio between Roman and medieval Wales.[30]

Houlder's popular guide gives a handy map of the site, reproduces a snake of gold (some six inches long) found there, and notes that traces of a fort were found (in 1972) at Pumsaint.[31] Dolau Cothi appears in a standard book on ancient mining, with photographs of the square-sided tunnels running eighty feet into the hillside.[32] Later writers may be dealt with as follows. Gerald of Wales refers to the commot of Caio as home of Gruffydd ap Rhys and Gwenllian, on whom he would be well-informed, since Gruffydd's sister Nest was Gerald's own grand-mother. He refers in veiled terms to how his pen 'quivers in his hand' as he thinks of the 'terrible vengeance exacted in our own times' by the king's troops on the subject people of Caio. This presumably refers to events after the disaster of Gwenllian's attack on Kidwelly (and her execu-tion on the battlefield) in early 1136.[33] Rivet and Smith gave the British-Latin name of the fort at Pumsaint (its importance underlined by Ptolemy's mention of it) as *Luentinum* 'washing-place', which they related to the washing of gold-bearing ores (perhaps correctly, though they were wrong in explaining the Welsh cognate *lludw* as 'rain': it means 'ashes'); Professor Peter Schrijver of

Munich has suggested to the writer that Gaulish *lautro* 'bath' and Middle Breton *louazr* 'trough' may here provide cognates.[34]

Bowen, though not mentioning Cynyr or Caio, stressed St David's associations with south Ceredigion (ruled by his father, Sant), especially his early education at Henfynyw (SN 4461).[35] Caio is eighteen miles south-east of Henfynyw (along the modern A 482), so would not be difficult of access from there. Wendy Davies cites Glanville Jones's paper; so, too, do Jenkins and Owen.[36] Simon Evans summed up what we know of Paulinus, who perhaps came from Llandingad (SN 7734), immediately east of Llandovery, though Evans admitted the Maesllanwrthwl inscription may be nothing to do with him.[37] Further light on the Dyfel son of Erbin mentioned in Glanville Jones's account of Caio is given by the *Mabinogion*. Dyfel would have lived in the early sixth century, and been the brother of the Vortipor who was attacked by Gildas, and whose tombstone can be seen in Carmarthen Museum.[38] So Dyfel was of the blood royal. If his brother was alive about 540, Dyfel would have been contemporary with the birth of St David about 520. These allusions provide further evidence for Caio's élite associations.

Progress on the Roman remains can now be followed in the journal *Britannia*. Most recently, a magnetometer survey of Pumsaint cricket pitch (SN 656405) revealed details of the east side of the Roman fort (which was almost square, covered 5.6 acres, had a rampart of turf and clay with double ditches, and showed seven phrases of construction in its interior buildings, dated within the period 75–150). The survey also revealed an associated *vicus* settlement and a substantial boundary feature overlain by what seemed to be a linear bath house.[39] As regards David's ancestry, the latest comment is by Dumville, who calls the story of David's conception 'an elaborate series of fictions' (no doubt it is). Yet he finds it odd that a prince of Ceredigion should be described as David's father. David's cult-centre is west Dyfed, not Ceredigion, and modern historians know of no medieval political need to 'claim' David for Ceredigion.[40] So it may be that, while David's pretensions to royal blood are shaky, his family associations really were with south Ceredigion, though this circumstance was played down by St Davids writers.

III

That concludes the second part of this chapter. It includes much that is familiar to archaeologists, but some things that will be less so. Now for our next part, on the caer of the *cawg* in the third of the *Four Branches of the Mabinogi*. It is a dramatic tale. The heroes Manawydan and Pryderi go out hunting from Arberth. By a nearby wood (*perth*) they confront a preternatural boar of 'shining white', which leads their hounds to a 'huge lofty caer all newly built, in a place where they had never seen either stone or building'. Against Manawydan's advice, Pryderi enters this fort, finds there 'a fountain with marble work around, and on the edge of the fountain a golden bowl fastened to four chains, and that upon a marble slab, and the chains ascending into the air, and he could see no end to them'. Transported by the beauty of the gold and workmanship of the bowl, Pryderi takes hold of it and is trapped by magic power. After waiting all day outside, Manawydan returns to Arberth, where his wife Rhiannon expresses scorn on his disloyalty to his friend, seeks out the fort from his directions, and is trapped there herself. When night comes, they and the fort vanish in a 'peal of thunder' and fall of mist. Only at the close of the tale are Pryderi and Rhiannon released from their magic captivity, when Manawydan outwits the sorcerer who has imprisoned them.[41]

How do we relate this strange tale to what we know of Caio? One thing must be made clear at once. Wherever the strange fort of the bowl was, it was nowhere near Caio. Manawydan and Pryderi set out from Arberth, and it is now agreed this was the farm of Arberth (SN 2046), a mile east of Cardigan. North of Arberth is Banc-y-Warren (an ancient mound by the main road from Cardigan to Aberystwyth), which is the Gorsedd Arberth of these tales.[42] The text says Manawydan and Pryderi saw the fort from the top of the mound, so presumably it was towards the sea and away from Arberth, though within walking distance (the text does not mention horses). Since it was a fort of the Other World (like the mound itself, scene of supernatural events), it would be vain to try and locate it further, or identify it with Crug Llwyn-llwyd (SN 2047) north of Banc-y-Warren.

Critics have said relatively little on this fort and its bowl. Gruffydd noted the folk-tale aspect of the treacherous bowl.[43] Stressing the Celtic Other World aspect, Loomis compared the episode with passages in French and Irish (neither of which mentions a bowl).[44] Jackson, like Gruffydd, related the the scene to international tales of persons who stick to a magic pot.[45] As regards etymology, Vendryes described Irish *cuach* 'cup, bowl' and Welsh *cawg* 'bowl' as cognates and native words, not borrowed from Latin.[46] Koch see the bowl as 'a reversal of the golden cup' of sovereignty in early Irish tradition.[47] McKenna cites this without comment.[48] Yet one may say it is not likely the author of the *Four Branches* would know of an allusion to sovereignty here. The tale of the golden bowl seems to have no ulterior significance. It is merely another instance of the author's appetite for marvels. There seems no reason to relate it to anything in Celtic mythology, though it may of course tell us something of the author's techniques of composition.

This brings us to our final part, where we try to fit together the above pieces of archaeological and other data. How do they add to our knowledge of Caio? There appear to be four conclusions here. First, the Caer Gawch where Cynyr lived within the commot of Caio has never been identified; but it seems reasonable to take it as the renamed Roman fort at Pumsaint. Such a building would be a formidable structure, useful as the court of a Celtic chieftain, Irish or Welsh; *caer* is the typical element for a

Roman camp in Welsh toponyms (Cardiff, Carmarthen, Caernarfon), and is sometimes qualified by the name of the chieftain or saint who lived there (Caergybi or Holyhead, Caerphilly, Caersws). Hence, surely, the Book of Llandaff's reference to Pumsaint Caercaiau. There is certainly no other structure (Roman or other) in the Caio region which deserves the name *caer*. So we may feel fairly certain that the fort discovered at Pumsaint in 1972 is Caer Gawch, home of Cynyr, a chieftain of Irish descent whom tradition asserted to be the father of St Non and grandfather of Wales's national saint. The very obscurity of Cynyr and Caer Gawch strengthens the case for this. As the tradition served no later political need, it was forgotten or ignored except by those around Caio, who cherished it into the fifteenth century and later. Archaeologists with their magnetometers at Pumsaint cricket pitch may feel fairly sure the Roman fort beneath the turf was called Caer Gawch in the post-Roman period.

Second, we can suggest how the fort gained its name. *Cawch* has no meaning in Welsh. The existence of Glen Quaich in Perthshire and Kinross, Cuaig in the West Highlands, and Coagh by Lough Neagh therefore point to influence from Irish. It seems that *cawch* is an attempt to represent Irish *cuach* 'bowl', referring not to potholes in a river, but rather to the situation of Pumsaint at the junction of the Cothi ('purger') and the Trwch ('boar'). The fort was situated in the hollow (obvious from the map) where these forceful rivers met. The name being Irish (like that Cynyr himself), Welsh scribes and others had difficulty with it. Hence Gerald of Wales's *Kaoc* and the Book of Llandaff's *kaircaiau*, the latter giving modern 'Caio'.

Third, Caio and the *Four Branches*. Ifor Williams long ago associated Caer Gawch with the author of these tales, thinking that traditions of Cynyr's home prompted the legend of the magic fort, with its perilous golden bowl. His reasoning seems confirmed by evidence within the tales that associates them with Gwenllian, who spent much of her married life at Caio.[49] If she took a local toponym as the basis for a fiction, it would shed light on her techniques of story-telling, especially as there is no other evidence for legends of the fort of the bowl in Welsh tradition. The story would begin with her (and was perhaps reused, minus the fort, in the *Mabinogion* romance of Owain). If so, Caer Gawch near Caio has become the caer of the *cawg* or bowl in the tale, and been transported sixty miles west to the outskirts of Cardigan. The author of the *Four Branches* had a passion for locating the narrative at real places (Aberffraw, Harlech, Caer Seint, Tomen y Mur, Rhuddlan Teifi, Glyn Cuch, and many other sites, often archaeological ones). With Caer Gawch, it seems a real toponym has been used, but moved from Carmarthenshire to west Ceredigion. (One might add that the nearby caves might also prompt a story of dangerous places, where one might be trapped, since such a story was recorded by Baring-Gould and Fisher from modern folklore at Caio. But that cannot be proved. Similarly, one would like to to think the river Twrch 'boar' at Pumsaint inspired the white boar of the *Four Branches*; which, however, use the word *baedd*, not *twrch*.) What is not in doubt is evidence associating Caer Gawch, Caio, Gwenllian, and the magic fort of the tale of Manawydan.

Fourth, gold. Here we must be negative. The *Four Branches* often mention gold. Pwyll sees gold plate in the Other World; an Irish king receives compensation of a gold dish as broad as his face; shoes of Spanish leather are decorated with gold; land, territory, or gold are offered as compensation for injury.[50] This complements references to gold in earlier Welsh sources.[51] It would be pleasant to think some of this gold came from mines near Caio. But nothing in the *Four Branches* implies this. Nor does Gerald of Wales mention gold at Caio, which one might expect him to do (he merely mentions its forests). So the gold that figures in the *Four Branches* probably did not come from Wales. Yet there is an allusion to gold from Ireland (a place the author knew well), found on battlefields (and not in the Wicklow Mountains).[52] So the *Four Branches* do show awareness in the early twelfth century of Ireland as a source of gold.

The above analysis therefore advances our knowledge of the Caio area in various ways. It suggests the Roman fort was occupied about 500 by Cynyr, who had an Irish name, and surely Irish followers. (If the Black Book of Carmarthen verse has any authority, he or his children might have had prince Dyfel son of Erbin as a neighbour.) Archaeologists may thus discover evidence for his post-Roman occupation at Pumsaint (re-use of Roman forts, by royal grant to monasteries, being well known).[53] Cynyr and his men may have described the depression in which Pumsaint lies by the Irish word *cuach* 'bowl; hollow', so that the fort was in later Welsh called *Caer Gawch* 'fort of the hollow' (perhaps giving modern *Gaeo*). If so, this Irish form would be on the fringe of Irish toponyms in south-west Wales as plotted by Melville Richards.[54] Cynyr may have been the father of St Non, who about 520 supposedly gave birth to St David. The evidence for this, faint as it is, is still stronger than that for David's father Sant and his place in the royal house of Ceredigion. It also accords with the persistent association of David and his mother with southern Ceredigion, which Caio lies just beyond. In the twelfth century Caer Gawch, by a kind of folk-etymology or place-name lore characteristic in the Celtic lands, perhaps suggested a tale of a fort with a magic bowl from the author of the *Four Branches of the Mabinogi*, who lived nearby, but who for the purposes of narrative relocated the magic fort near Cardigan.

In short, it appears that the fort at Pumsaint brings together traditions of St David and the *Four Branches of the Mabinogi*, which together provide the major early narratives to come out of south-west Wales. It also brings together in what seems to be a coherent way a variety of archaeological, linguistic, and historical evidence from ancient and medieval Wales, which points to post-Roman use of the fort at Pumsaint, perhaps by an Irish chieftain who gained fame as the father and grandfather of saints.

Notes

1. Baring-Gould and Fisher, ii. 289–90, iii. 225–6.
2. Lloyd, *History*, 153–4.
3. Ifor Williams, 'Nodiadau Ieithyddol', 256–60.
4. Wade-Evans, 71. For help with this text the writer thanks Dr Salvador Ryan of NUI, Maynooth.
5. Watson, 542.
6. Coates and Breeze, 227–8.
7. R. T. Jenkins, 108.
8. *Pedeir Keinc*, 238.
9. Lloyd-Jones, 263.
10. Foster, 218–19; Breeze, 107–8.
11. Wendy Davies, *Llandaff Charters*, 13, 123.
12. Lloyd, *Story*, 8–9.
13. Chadwick, 'Intellectual Life', 137.
14. *Early Welsh Genealogical Tracts*, 54.
15. Bowen, *Saints*, 183.
16. *Trioedd*, 37, 307–8.
17. Padel, 50, 132.
18. Dumville, 27.
19. *Welsh Life*, 27; Breeze, 67–8; *Gwaith Ieuan ap Rhydderch*, 177.
20. Samuel Lewis, 236–7.
21. Lloyd, *History*, 267, 435.
22. Collingwood and Myres, 229.
23. A. H. Williams, 60.
24. Randall, 89–90.
25. Charlesworth, 51.
26. They are items 33 and 139–41 in Nash-Williams.
27. Richmond, 157.
28. Frere, 283.
29. Liversedge, 141, 209–10.
30. G. R. J. Jones, at 311–20.
31. Houlder, 167–8.
32. Healy, 52, plate 20.
33. Gerald of Wales, 139.
34. Lewis and Pedersen, 12; Rivet and Smith, 400; cf. Dark, 98.
35. Bowen, *St David*, 11–16.
36. Wendy Davies, *Wales*, 44, 45, 48–9; Jenkins and Owen, 'Welsh Marginalia', 52–3.
37. *Welsh Life*, 35–6.
38. Thomas Jones, 123; *Culhwch and Olwen*, 81; cf. R. Geraint Gruffydd, 'Edmyg Dinbych', 13–14.
39. Burnham et al., 372–3.
40. Dumville, *Saint David*, 28–9.

41. Jones and Jones, 45–7.
42. W. J. Gruffydd, *Rhiannon*, 18 n. 1; *Pwyll*, 24; Breeze, *Medieval Welsh Literature*, 69, 71.
43. W. J. Gruffydd, *Rhiannon*, 77.
44. Loomis, 168–70.
45. Jackson, *International Popular Tale*, 104.
46. Vendryes, 258–9.
47. Koch, 35.
48. McKenna, 'Education', 115.
49. Cf. Roberts, 'Where Were the *Four Branches of the Mabinogi* Written?', 61–75.
50. Jones and Jones, 6, 28, 65–6, 74.
51. Davies, *Wales*, 48–9.
52. Jones and Jones, 40; Mac Cana, *Branwen*, 36 n. 3.
53. Cf. Alcock, 326; Thomas, 33–4; Rees, *Caerphilly Castle*, 2–4; Victory, 42–3.
54. Davies, *Wales*, 88.

Some Recent Views of the
Four Branches

The previous chapters have made plain what can be inferred from the text of the *Four Branches* on their origins and provenance. But does it stand up to criticism? Is it consistent with research on the *Mabinogi* published independently in the last few years?

I

It may be said at once that those who demand complete certainty on the point will never be satisfied. In matters of historical analysis and literary judgement, no such proof can be expected that will resemble those of the physical sciences. A similar point was made by A. E. Housman in his paper 'The Application of Thought to Textual Criticism'. He wrote as follows. If chemists wish to find whether a mixture of sulphur, saltpetre, and charcoal is explosive, they need only apply a match. If doctors wish to find what diseases, if any, a new drug will cure, they need only give it to patients all round and notice which die and which recover. Textual critics have no such good fortune. 'Our conclusions regarding the truth or falsehood of a manuscript reading can never be confirmed or corrected by an equally decisive test; for the only equally decisive test would be the production of the author's authograph.'[1] As we are unlikely ever to have a copy of the *Four Branches* with the autograph of Gwenllian, there are perhaps some who will never accept (and may perhaps even deny) that the *Four Branches* are the work of Gwenllian.

It may be, however, that those who do so will become fewer as time goes on, stating their views with less confidence; or merely retreating into silence. In the meantime discussion can be advanced by a look at some recent work. Here five papers of criticism and research may be chosen as a sample of current thinking. In order of official publication date, they are by Fiona Winward, William Parker, Ned Sturzer, Paul Russell, and Catherine McKenna.

II

We begin with Fiona Winward. There need be no dispute about much of her discussion, or its careful analysis of the women of the *Four Branches* as unmarried, married, estranged, or mothers. The paper begins by citing others on the women of the *Four Branches* as having power over their own lives and thus being subjects for interpretation as women in the rest of the *Mabinogion* (for the most part the stock-figures of folktale) are not. This is true. But two points may be debated. First, Winward's citation of Roberta Valente's statement that 'men have more lines of dialogue' is misleading and sometimes false.[2] In the tale of Pwyll, when Arawn and his wife are in bed, we have fourteen lines of the thoughts and words of Arawn's wife, and eleven of those of Arawn; and it is Arawn's wife who has the advantage. She gives her husband short shrift when he tells a weak falsehood, with her 'Shame on me if since a year from yesternight, from the time we were enfolded in the bedclothes, there has been either delight or converse between us, or that thou hast turned thy face towards me, let alone anything that would be more than that between us.' And Arawn has to admit the truth. When Gwawl first comes to the court of Hefeydd, Pwyll speaks in fourteen lines, Rhiannon in fifty-six, and Hefeydd himself (more marginal than Emma's Mr Woodhouse) none. Rhiannon, of course, dominates the situation. When we come to Teyrnon, he speaks in eighteen lines, his wife in seventeen, and she also gets her way. These singular facts speak for themselves.

Second and finally, the conclusions to the paper. Here there can be no agreement. The present writer thinks no man would have written the *Four Branches*: Fiona Windward is sure they are the work of a man. Naturally it is true that the women of these narratives exist in a male-dominated society or patriarchy; and that Queen Anne is dead. What matters is that are features of the texts which have no parallel in any text known to be the work of a male writer. There are also serious mistatements even as regards the text. For example, we are told that 'Rhiannon is spirited and powerful as a single woman, and defeatist and briefly nameless as a wife and mother'.[3] Let us refer to the text. When Pryderi is trapped in the magic caer, Manawydan returns home without him, and confesses all to Rhiannon. Her reaction is swift. '"Faith," said Rhiannon, "a bad comrade hast thou been, but a good comrade hast thou lost." And with that word out she went', to seek her son. This appears a strange kind of spiritless defeatism. Again, we are told that the author loses interest in her when 'as a wife and mother, she loses her capacity for adventure, having fulfilled her function.'[4] But there is no need to explain this in terms of patriarchy; any more than one need explain the young unmarried state of Jane Austen's heroines by structures of male domination in Regency England. A period of life in which one is relatively free and the future is uncertain is of more interest for the purposes of narrative than one in which the future is relatively certain, and there is in any case less of it.

As for the comment on the curious preoccupation of the *Four Branches* with motherhood, including child-bearing, wet-nursing, childlessness, fostering, and the upbringing of children, one may speak to the point. Fiona Windward discounts this with the comment 'it is very much the patriarchal attitude to motherhood that is being portrayed', the mothers being portrayed 'from a male perspective'.[5] This is unconvincing. Let us take wet-nursing. This occurs not once but twice. In the first branch Teyrnon's wife brings women into league with her, and the boy is 'nursed in the court' till he is a year old. Those women supplied milk. We are told the boy is nursed until he is two. In the fourth branch Gwydion finds an infant boy, takes him to the town (Caernarfon?), 'where he knew there was a woman with breasts. And he made a bargain with the woman to suckle the child', whose growth is then described.[6]

In pre-industrial societies children were commonly breast-fed until they were two (as was often the case here in Spain during the civil war). A grim aspect of this is revealed by recent archaeological work at Wharram Percy (SE 8564) in the Yorkshire Wolds. Excavation of medieval burials there shows the death rate of children rose sharply after they reached the age of two. The implication is obvious. Before that age they were fed from the breast, and were spared contact with sources of disease; once suckled, they would drink water that was contaminated, and so would catch fever and die.[7]

One allusion to breast-feeding may be regarded as adventitious. Two looks like matriarchy. Why this interest in such a subject, which the author of the *Four Branches* is aware of as something lasting two years? And where can Fiona Winward show any text by a male writer with so unusual a concern? If this evidence is to be taken as counting for nothing, much of our literature should be expected to show similar concerns; since most literature is written by men. But a easier explanation stares us in the face. Entities are not to be multiplied; and critics should avoid adding epicycles to preserve the appearance of male authorship when the hypothesis of female authorship simplifies matters so greatly. It is sometimes hard to change one's mind on what one has always been told, and for some it is impossible. But any history of science or medicine will spell out the dangers of failing to do this, despite the natural advantages of the conservative attitude in saving one the trouble of thought.

III

After Fiona Winward, William Parker, in a paper dated winter 2002 (though actually appearing in June 2004).[8] This begins boldly by affirming a date for the *Mabinogi* in the late twelfth century. It then examines the debate on Dyfed *vs* Gwynedd authorship, quite properly citing the work of Bollard, Ford, Gantz, and Roberts for dislodging the old hypothesis of an original saga on the Dyfed hero Pryderi. So the authorial plinth is left empty for a Gwynedd writer. At this point, however, we begin to register disagreement. We are told that 'The fulsome praise of the Dyfed countryside in the third branch and the sympathy for the beaten men of Deheubarth in the fourth are probably just as easily explained in terms of the literary detail than as indicators of regional bias.' This explanation explains nothing. If it were correct, why the author's silence on other parts of Wales? Why no fulsome praise for the beauties of Powys or Glamorgan? Sympathy being precious, most people ration it, including our author. One has a right to expect a reason why the words in the narrative appear as they do, and not other. But Parker here offers no reason at all.

Parker gives corroborative detail for his Gwynedd author with useful maps of places mentioned in the stories. He locates forty toponyms. Such an initiative deserves praise. Unfortunately, his map has grave flaws. It locates Arberth in south Pembrokeshire, which cannot be so. All informed scholars must follow T. Llew Jone's paper of 1991 which locates it a mile east of Cardigan, where Banc-y-Warren is the mound of Arberth from which Pwyll first saw Rhiannon, and where the place name still appears on Ordnance Survey maps with Nant Arberth, further to the east. Parker locates the valley of the Cuch too far to the east and omits Penn Llwyn Diarwya, apparently a small hillfort a mile north of where the Cuch meets the Teifi. He omits Preseli, where Pwyll met his men. Once these toponyms are properly located, we see a significant cluster in the lower Teifi basin. Parker's failure to do this means that, although two clusters of toponyms in Gwynedd are evident (one south of Caernarfon, the other in the Portmadoc-Ffestiniog region), a third cluster near Cardigan does not appear. So the way is open for a corrected version of his maps using the grid references established earlier in this book. Yet it is worth repeating that Parker's maps are a step in the right direction, showing at a glance what one might laboriously deduce from a list. His innovative approach to *Mabinogi* studies is to be welcomed.

However, he goes on to spoil this helpful contribution with a massive non-sequitur. Because of these local names 'it seems more likely than not that the final redaction of the *Mabinogi* took place in a definable area of north-west Wales'. This is like saying that the final redaction of *Ulysses* took place in Dublin. Having made one non-sequitur, he provides another, that this geographical familiarity allows identification of the audience and patrons of the stories. (One imagines another and future Parker on a distant planet identifying the audience and patronage of Joyce's *Ulysses* as Irish, and proposing that the book appeared with a subsidy from the newly-founded Irish Free State.)

Logic lets us go wrong with confidence. Having made assumptions for which there is no basis, William Parker works from them to offer some quite remarkable conclusions. Specifically, within an absolute time limit of 1066–1225 (the latter being the approximate date of the MS Peniarth 6 fragments), he argues for a dating of 1164–1197 as the most likely period of composition, 'on the basis of the political-geographical assumptions of the text'.[9] He thinks the tales were written in 'a Caernarvonshire court sympathetic to the ambitions of the young Llywelyn ap Iorwerth (latterly Llywelyn Fawr, Prince of Wales)', who died in 1240.

This is vapourware. Let us look at the arguments for this. First, the role of London. Parker is right in seeing how London appears in the stories as a centre of political power. That surely locates the texts after 1066. The

Confessor was crowned at Winchester, but Harold, the Conqueror, William Rufus, and Henry I were crowned at London. (The significance of the ceremony was not lost on Stephen. Henry I died on 1 December 1135, when Stephen was in France. On hearing the news he crossed the Channel and was crowned at Westminster on or about 22 December, events happening 'in the twinkling of an eye'.) But Parker's view that the unidiomatic and Latinate phrase *ardyrchawc o goron Llundein* 'exalted with the crown of London', applied in the second branch to Bendigeidfran, pushes the date of composition of the *Four Branches* to after 1136, when Geoffrey of Monmouth used the phrase in his *History of the Kings of Britain*, perches a mountain on a pinhead. Two things may be said against it. There is no reason to think Geoffrey coined the expression; and, if the *Four Branches* post-date Geoffrey, it is extraordinary that they show no other influence from him (particularly when his writings found readers in Wales so soon after publication). The *Four Branches* never so much as mention Arthur; which is curious, if they are as late as William Parker thinks. As for the view, elaborately expressed, that political relations of North and South in the tales mirror events of the late twelfth century, it may briefly be said there is nothing in it that compels assent, and it creates difficulties for the dating of the later *Mabinogion* texts, profuse in romance loanwords (as the *Four Branches* are not), which on this basis would have to be pushed well into the thirteenth century, a view few commentators will be ready to accept.

Finally, Parker's comments in a postscript on this writer's attribution of the stories to a woman writer, who can be taken as Gwenllian. This has special value in drawing attention to exciting theoretical writings by feminist writers, particularly Katherine Millersdaughter. Readers are recommended to turn to these works for themselves. But as regards the present book three things may be said, as follows. First, the assignment of the *Mabinogi* to a woman writer is not an 'assertion' (still less 'speculation'). It is a reasonable deduction from features of the text which have no parallel in the works of male writers, but are paralleled in the work of women writers. Second, an argument for the dating and provenance of a text must be complete and coherent. It must be able to account for all aspects of the work at hand, palaeographical, linguistic, literary, and historical. Third, it should also be capable of being knocked down. If false, it should be possible to prove this on objective grounds. The analogies with evidence given by informed witnesses in a court of law are here pertinent. A barrister will soon pick holes in a story which is false, and thereby demolish it. But a story which is true will be coherent, and will be rich in corroborative detail. It will not fall down in the face of hostile questioning. On such a basis we may also exercise our judgement in our literary and historical investigations, where we may distinguish arguments that collapse under criticism, and those that do not. (As for the recent view put forward by one professor of Welsh, that we do not know the date of the *Four Branches* within the widest limits, and therefore discussion is pointless, this may be regarded as mindlessness.)

IV

Next, the papers by Ned Sturzer, Paul Russell, and Catherine McKenna.[10] None of these refers to the work of this writer, though their authors all kindly sent him offprints on request. Sturzer's paper lists supposed inconsistencies within the *Four Branches* in order to divide them amongst different authors. When Teyrnon notices that the infant Pryderi resembles Pwyll, this is accounted for by saying that Teyrnon had once been Pwyll's vassal, and so knew what he looked like. Sturzer find this unconvincing, since Gwent is far from Dyfed, and Pwyll is 'no Arthur attracting followers from afar'. He therefore regards it as an interpolation by another hand.[11] One might rightly take it showing the seams of storytelling, though such things are found in the greatest writers (the improbable coincidences and meetings in Dickens). But Sturzer's point bears another implication. If Pwyll is so minor a prince, why should the author describe a Gwent lord as his former vassal? Because the author thought all South Wales should be under the rule of Dyfed.

His further comment on the rivers in the second branch that overflowed to create the Irish Sea is surely post-authorial, and reminds us of that our text is not as secure as we might wish it. Yet the loadstones at the bottom of the Liffey, which suck down invading craft, are less easily dismissed. The author had a narrator's interest in processes and even technology (capture in a bag of food, smearing with the blood of dogs, bellows to make an iron house white-hot, kneading at the dough-trough, blows from a butcher's knife, starlings as messengers, the making of shields, shoes, and saddles, the creation of steeds, hounds, saddles, ships, and shoes by magic, a novel way to murder a husband). Loadstones would be in keeping with these.

As for the admittedly numerous further inconsistencies, none of these amounts to a case for different authors, particularly given the consistencies of style and character-ization recognized by almost all recent critics. Sturzer is out on a limb here. He notes that at the end of the third branch we hear of a spell cast on the seven cantrefs of Dyfed, when Pryderi at the close of the first is also ruler of Ystrad Tywi and Ceredigion (in the fourth he added Morgannwg to his domains). Sturzer concludes that the author of the third branch did not write the first or fourth.[12] Seen from the United States of America, where the emphasis on union is strong, as underlined by the events of 1861–5 (not least in Chattanooga), such a view is logical. But it makes little sense in medieval Wales, with a strong sense of local loyalties, and where a chaos of conflicting laws and jurisdictions continued up to Henry VIII's acts of union. Llwyd mab Cil Coed therefore sends his curse against Dyfed, the ancient ancestral territory of the ruling house; he is not concerned with later additions to their lands.

Again, Sturzer finds an anomaly in the third branch, where the protagonists travel to England, a land of towns with guilds of craftsmen, quite at variance with the supposed ancient Celtic world in which the action normally takes place. He finds the allusions there to clerk, priest, and bishop similarly incongruous, as also the mention of twenty-four pounds in cash.[13] But few are likely to agree with him on these points. Many will see them as no more than the inconsistencies any storyteller might be guilty of (if guilt is the right word); like the curious silence of Macbeth and Lady Macbeth on their children. Nor does one detect a different hand in the characterization of the third branch, or in the language they use to each other, the emphasis on marvels and objects of beauty, or the love of Dyfed. If the third branch is a weaker thing than the others, it is perhaps because the author had used up the cream of narrative concerning Dyfed in the first branch.

V

Finally, the papers by Russell and McKenna. For present purposes, Paul Russell's paper is effectively a review of *150 Jahre: 'Mabinogion'* (Tübingen, 2001), a book which makes no mention whatever of the present writer's work on the *Four Branches* or indeed on anything else. It thus has value as containing independent accounts of the subject. The papers in it here most relevant are by Thomas Charles-Edwards on textual transmission, Patrick Sims-Williams on Clynnog, and Ceridwen Lloyd-Morgan on gender and violence. As regards the *Mabinogi*, the main conclusion of Charles-Edwards is the reassuring one of the relative stability of its text compared with, for example, that of *Peredur* or the laws. He is unsure whether this followed a fluid tradition or whether the tales assumed 'a fixed, canonical status almost immediately'.[14] If, of course, the arguments of this book are accepted, the answer would be the second. They would be the literary work of an individual of high status and would be treated with the respect that would entail. In this context may be noted the evidence set out in chapter one of the present book, associating the textual tradition of the *Four Branches* with Dyfed (even though two of them deal with Gwynedd), and specifically with the Lord Rhys (1132–97). As for Sims-Williams's question of a link with Clynnog, this has been emphatically rejected in chapter six. There is not a shred of real evidence for it, and ample evidence against it. Dr Russell says nothing on Ceridwen Lloyd-Morgan's consideration of the considerable amount of male violence against women in the *Four Branches* (Rhiannon's humiliation, Branwen's ill-treatment by the royal butcher, the rape of Goewin). But it may be said that all are women of integrity and are all vindicated. The reason for their suffering comes to light and they are find themselves morally justified. The same is not true of Aranrhod or Blodeuedd, a bad mother and a bad wife. Aranrhod is outwitted and her intentions frustrated; Blodeuedd's career ends in disaster. Dr Lloyd-Morgan is curiously silent on the nature of the author of these tales, in which women play so prominent a part.

Professor Catherine McKenna, now of Harvard University, deals with the fourth branch at length in the American way, but without proving anything in particular.[15] Like Dr Russell, Professor McKenna makes no reference whatever to the writer's views on the *Mabinogi*.

VI

And so we reach the conclusion, in which (rather as in Johnson's *Rasselas*) nothing is concluded. At the moment there is no agreement among Celticists worldwide on the origins of the *Four Branches of the Mabinogi*, despite the millions of pounds and dollars spent on professorial salaries and research grants to achieve this end. Naturally, those who have read this book will have found a complete, detailed, and circumstantial explanation for the origin, authorship, and provenance of these tales. It is submitted that this explanation is compelling, cogent, and very simple. When, therefore, scholars in centuries to come look back at this whole debate, involving highly-trained professionals at many universities, they will surely think that many amongst them were sadly deceived. But on just which of them were so misled, the reader may determine.

Notes

1. Housman, *Classical Papers*, 1062.
2. Winward, 'Some Aspects', 79.
3. Winward, 'Some Aspects', 101.
4. Winward, 'Some Aspects', 101.
5. Windward, 'Some Aspects', 105, 106.
6. Jones and Jones, *Mabinogion*, 20–1, 64.
7. Cf. Beresford and Hurst, 'Wharram Percy', 72.
8. Parker, 'Gwynedd', 365–96.
9. Parker 'Gwynedd', 370.
10. Sturzer, 'Inconsistencies', 127–42; Russell, 'Recent Work', 59–72; McKenna, 'Revising Math', 95–117.
11. Sturzer, 'Inconsistencies', 128.
12. Sturzer, 'Inconsistencies', 135.
13. Sturzer, 'Inconsistencies', 139.
14. Russell, 'Texts in Contexts', 62.
15. McKenna, 'Revising Math', 96–117.

Bibliography

Edited Books

Aislinge Meic Con Glinne, ed. K. H. Jackson (Dublin, 1990).

Branwen Uerch Lyr, ed. D. S. Thomson (Dublin, 1961).

Celtic Arthurian Material, ed. Ceridwen Lloyd-Morgan (Cambridge, 2004).

The Classical Papers of A. E. Housman, ed. J. Diggle and F. R. D. Goodyear (Cambridge, 1972).

Culhwch and Olwen, ed. Rachel Bromwich and D. Simon Evans (Cardiff, 1992).

Cyfranc Lludd a Llefelys, ed. B. F. Roberts (Dublin, 1975).

Dictionary of Welsh Biography (London, 1959).

Early Welsh Genealogical Tracts, ed. P. C. Bartrum (Cardiff, 1966).

English Historical Documents c.500–1042, ed. Dorothy Whitelock, 2nd edn (London, 1979).

Geiriadur Prifysgol Cymru (Caerdydd, 1950–2002).

Gwaith Bleddyn Ddu, ed. Iestyn Daniel (Aberystwyth, 1994).

Gwaith Dafydd ap Gwilym ed. Thomas Parry (Caerdydd, 1952).

Gwaith Ieuan ap Rhydderch, ed. R. Iestyn Daniel (Aberystwyth, 2003).

Gwaith Llywelyn Fardd I, ed. Morfydd Owen (Aberystwyth, 1994).

Hamlet, ed. Harold Jenkins (London, 1982).

Historia Gruffud vab Kenan, ed. D. Simon Evans (Caerdydd, 1977).

Llawysgrif Hendregadredd, ed. John Morris-Jones and T. H. Parry-Williams (Caerdydd, 1933).

The Mabinogi: A Book of Essays, ed. C. W. Sullivan (New York, 1996).

The Merry Wives of Windsor, ed. T. W. Craik (Oxford, 1989).

Mesca Ulad, ed. J. Carmichael Watson (Dublin, 1941).

The Oxford Book of Welsh Verse, ed. Thomas Parry (Oxford, 1962).

Pedeir Keinc y Mabinogi, ed. Ifor Williams (Caerdydd, 1930).

Peniarth 76, ed. E. S. Roberts and W. J. Gruffydd (Caerdydd, 1927).

The Poems of Taliesin, ed. Ifor Williams (Dublin, 1968).

Pwyll Pendeuic Dyuet, ed. R. L. Thomson (Dublin, 1957).

Táin Bó Cúailnge from the Book of Leinster, ed. Cecile O'Rahilly (Dublin, 1967).

Trioedd Ynys Prydain, ed. Rachel Bromwich, 2nd edn (Cardiff, 1978).

The Welsh Law of Women, ed Dafydd Jenkins and Morfydd Owen (Cardiff, 1980).

The Welsh Life of St David, ed. D. Simon Evans (Cardiff, 1988).

Other Publications

Alcock, Leslie, *Arthur's Britain* (London, 1971).

Baring-Gould, Sabine and Fisher, John, *The Lives of the British Saints* (London, 1907–13).

Beresford, M. W. and Hurst, J. G., 'Wharram Percy: A Case Study in Microtopography', in *English Medieval Settlement*, ed. P. H. Sawyer (London, 1979), 52–85.

Binchy, D. A., *Celtic and Anglo-Saxon Kingship* (Oxford, 1970).

Boon, G. C., *Segonium Roman Fort*, 2nd edn (London, 1963).

Bowen, E. G., *Saints, Seaways, and Settlements in the Celtic Lands*, 2nd edn (Cardiff, 1977).

——, *The St David of History* (Aberystwyth, 1982).

Breeze, A. C., *Medieval Welsh Literature* (Dublin, 1997).

——, 'Did a Woman Write the *Four Branches of the*

Mabinogi?', *Studi Medievali*, xxxiii (1997), 679–705.

——, 'Politics and the *Four Branches of the Mabinogi'*, *Memoria y Civilización*, ii (1999), 243–60.

——, 'Hywel ab Owain Gwynedd (d. 1170) and the *Four Branches of the Mabinogi'*, in *Feilscribhínn Ghearóid Mhic Eoin*, ed. Donall Ó Baoill and Donncha Ó hAodha (Dublin, 2009), 123–34.

——, 'Welsh Tradition and the Baker's Daughter in *Hamlet'*, *Notes and Queries*, ccxlvii (2002), 199–200.

——, 'The *Four Branches of the Mabinogi* in Our Time', *Voprosy Filologii*, xvii/2 (2004), 27–34.

Bromwich, Rachel, 'The Character of the Early Welsh Tradition', in *Studies in Early British History*, ed. Nora Chadwick (Cambridge, 1954), 83–136.

——, *Aspects of the Poetry of Dafydd ap Gwilym* (Cardiff, 1986).

Brown, R. Allen, et al., *The History of the King's Works: The Middle Ages* (London, 1963).

Bullock-Davies, Constance, *Professional Interpreters and the Matter of Britain* (Cardiff, 1966).

Burnham, B. C., et al., 'Roman Britain in 1999: Sites Explored', *Britannia*, xxxi (2000), 372–431.

Byrne, F. J., *Irish Kings and High-Kings* (London, 1973).

Chadwick, H. M. and Chadwick, Nora, *The Growth of Literature: The Ancient Literatures of Europe* (Cambridge, 1932).

Chadwick, Nora, 'Intellectual Life in West Wales in the Last Days of the Celtic Church', in *Studies in the Early British Church*, ed. Nora Chadwick (Cambridge, 1958), 121–82.

Charlesworth, M. P., *The Lost Province* (Cardiff, 1949).

Clancy, J. P., *The Earliest Welsh Poetry* (London, 1970).

Clarke, H. B., *Dublin c.840 to c.1540* (Dublin, 1978).

Coates, Richard and Breeze, Andrew, *Celtic Voices, English Places* (Stamford, 2000).

Collingwood, R. G. and Myres, J. N. L., *Roman Britain and the English Settlements*, 2nd edn (Oxford, 1937).

Dafydd ap Gwilym, *Fifty Poems*, tr. H. I. Bell and David Bell (London, 1942).

——, *A Selection of Poems*, tr. Rachel Bromwich (Llandysul, 1982).

Daniel, Glyn, 'Introduction', in *Prehistoric and Early Wales*, ed. Glyn Daniel and I. Ll. Foster (London, 1965), 1–15.

Daniel, Iestyn, 'The Date, Origin, and Authorship of "The Mabinogion" in the Light of *Ymborth yr Enaid*', *Journal of Celtic Studies*, iv (2004), 117–52.

Dark, K. R., *Civitas to Kingdom* (Leicester, 1994).

Davies, Pennar, *Rhwng Chwedl a Chredo* (Caerdydd, 1966).

Davies, R. R., *Wales 1063–1415* (Oxford, 1987).

Davies, Sioned, *Crefft y Cyfarwydd* (Caerdydd, 1995).

——, *The Mabinogion* (Oxford, 2007).

Davies, Wendy, *The Llandaff Charters* (Aberystwyth, 1977).

——, *Wales in the Early Middle Ages* (Leicester, 1982).

——, *Patterns of Power in Early Wales* (Oxford, 1990).

de Paor, Áine, 'The Common Authorship of some Book of Leinster Texts', *Ériu*, ix (1921), 118–46.

Dillon, Myles, *Early Irish Literature* (Chicago, 1948).

Dumville, D. N., *Saint David of Wales* (Cambridge, 2001).

Echard, Siân, *Arthurian Narrative in the Latin Tradition* (Cambridge, 1998).

Erlikhman, V. V., *Mabinogion: Volshebnye Legendy Uel'sa* ([Moscow,] 1995).

Finke, Laurie A., *Women's Writing in English: Medieval England* (London, 1999).

Flanagan, Marie-Therese, *Irish Society, Anglo-Norman Settlers, Angevin Kingship* (Oxford, 1989).

——, '*Historia Gruffud vab Kenan* and the Origins of Balrothery, Co. Dublin', *Cambrian Medieval Celtic Studies*, xxviii (1994), 71–94.

Flower, Robin, *Catalogue of Irish Manuscripts in the British Museum, ii* (London, 1926).

Ford, P. K., '*Branwen*: A Study of the Celtic Affinities', *Studia Celtica*, xxii–xxiii (1987), 29–41.

Foster, I. Ll., 'The Book of the Anchorite', *Proceedings of the British Academy*, xxxvi (1950), 197–226.

Frere, S. S., *Britannia* (London, 1967).

Gerald of Wales, *The Journey Through Wales* (Harmondsworth, 1978).

Griffiths, R. A., 'The Making of Medieval Ceredigion', *Ceredigion*, xi/2 (1990), 97–133.

Gruffydd, R. Geraint, '*Edmyg Dinbych*': *Cerdd Lys Gynnar o Ddyfed* (Aberystwyth, 2002).

Gruffydd, W. J., *Math vab Mathonwy* (Cardiff, 1928).

——, *Rhiannon* (Cardiff, 1953).

Haycock, Marged, 'Dylan Ail Ton', *Ysgrifau Beirniadol*, xiii (1985), 26–38.

Healy, J. F., *Mining and Metallurgy in the Greek and Roman World* (London, 1978).

Houlder, Christopher, *Wales: An Archaeological Guide* (London, 1974).

Hughes, Ian, '*Math fab Mathonwy* a Gwydion fab Dôn', *Dwned*, v (1999), 9–21.

Huws, Daniel, '*Llyfr Gwyn Rhydderch*', *Cambridge Medieval Celtic Studies*, xxi (1991), 1–37.

——, *Llyfrau Cymraeg 1250–1400* (Aberystwyth, 1992).

Jackson, K. H., *The International Popular Tale and Early Welsh Tradition* (Cardiff, 1961).

——, *A Celtic Miscellany*, 2nd edn (Harmondsworth, 1971).

Jarman, A. O. H., '*Pedeir Cainc y Mabinogi*', in *Y Traddodiad Rhyddiaith yn yr Oesau Canol*, ed. Geraint Bowen (Llandysul, 1974), 83–142.

Jenkins, Dafydd and Owen, Morfydd, 'The Welsh Marginalia in the Lichfield Gospels', *Cambridge Medieval Celtic Studies*, v (1983), 37–66.

Jenkins, R. T., *Yr Apêl at Hanes* ([Wrexham,] 1930).

Jones, Gwyn and Jones, Thomas, *The Mabinogion* (London, 1949).

Jones, G. R. J., 'Post-Roman Wales', in *The Agrarian History of England and Wales: AD 43–1042*, ed. H. P. R. Finberg (Cambridge, 1972), 281–382.

Jones, G. V., 'Llech Gronw', *Llên Cymru*, xvii/1–2 (1992), 131–3.

Jones, Thomas, 'The Black Book of Carmarthen "Stanzas of the Graves"', *Proceedings of the British Academy*, liii (1967), 97–137.

Jones, T. Llew, 'Banc y Warin, Y Crug Mawr, Gorsedd Arberth', *Llafar Gwlad*, xxxvi (1991), 6–7.

Koch, J. T., 'A Welsh Window on the Iron Age' in *Cambridge Medieval Celtic Studies*, xiv (1987), 17–52.

Lewis, Henry and Pedersen, Holger, *A Concise Comparative Celtic Grammar* (Göttingen, 1937).

Lewis, Samuel, *A Topographical Dictionary of Wales*, 3rd edn (London, 1844).

Lewis, C. W., 'The Literary Tradition of Morgannwg', in *Glamorgan County History: The Middle Ages*, ed. T. B. Pugh (Cardiff, 1971), 449–554.

Liversedge, Joan, *Britain in the Roman Empire* (London, 1968).

Lloyd, J. E., *A History of Wales* (London, 1911).

——, *The Story of Ceredigion* (Cardiff, 1937).

Lloyd-Jones, John, *Geirfa Barddoniaeth Gynnar Gymraeg* (Caerdydd, 1931–63).

Lloyd-Morgan, Ceridwen, 'The Branching Tree of Medieval Narrative: Welsh *Cainc* and French *Branche*' in *Romance Reading on the Book*, ed. Jennifer Fellows et al. (Cardiff, 1996), 36–50.

Loomis, R. S., *Wales and the Arthurian Legend* (Cardiff, 1956).

Mac Cana, Proinsias, *Branwen Daughter of Llŷr* (Cardiff, 1958).

——, *The Mabinogi* (Cardiff, 1977).

——, *The Mabinogi*, 2nd edn (Cardiff, 1992).

Mac Eoin, Gearóid, 'The Dating of Middle Irish Texts', *Proceedings of the British Academy*, lxviii (1982), 109–37.

Mac Gearailt, Uáitéar, 'The Edinburgh Text of *Mesca Ulad*', *Ériu*, xxxvii (1986), 133–79.

——, '*Cath Ruis na Ríg* and Twelfth-Century Literature and Oral Tradition', *Zeitschrift für celtische Philologie*, xliv (1991), 128–53.

——, 'The Language of Some Late Middle Irish Texts in the Book of Leinster', *Studia Hibernica*, xxvi (1991–2), 167–216.

——, 'The Relationship of Recensions II and III of the *Táin*', in *Ulidia*, ed. J. P. Mallory and Gerard Stockman (Belfast, 1994), 55–70.

Maund, Kari, *Ireland, Wales, and England in the Eleventh Century* (Woodbridge, 1991).

McKenna, Catherine, 'The Education of Manawydan', in *Ildánach, Ildírech*, ed. John Carey et al. (Andover, 1999), 101–30.

——, 'Revising Math: Kingship in the Fourth Branch of the *Mabinogi*', *Cambrian Medieval Celtic Studies*, xlvi (2003), 95–117.

Miles, Brent, '*Branwen*: A Reconsideration of the German and Norse Analogues', *Cambrian Medieval Celtic Studies*, lii (2006), 13–48.

Nash-Williams, V. E., *The Early Christian Monuments of Wales* (Cardiff, 1950).

Ó Concheanainn, Tomás, 'The Manuscript Tradition of *Mesca Ulad*', *Celtica*, xix (1987), 13–30.

Ó Corráin, Donncha, *Ireland before the Normans* (Dublin, 1972).

Ó Néill, Pádraig, 'The Latin Colophon to the "Táin Bó Cuailgne" in the Book of Leinster', *Celtica*, xxiii (1999), 269–75.

O'Rahilly, Cecile, *Ireland and Wales* (London, 1924).

O'Rahilly, T. F., *Early Irish History and Mythology* (Dublin, 1946).

Owen, Morfydd, 'Shame and Reparation: Women's Place in the Kin', in *The Welsh Law of Women*, ed. Dafydd Jenkins and Morfydd Owen (Cardiff, 1980), 40–60.

Padel, O. J., *A Popular Dictionary of Cornish Place Names* (Penzance, 1988).

Parker, William, 'Gwynedd, Ceredigion, and the Political Geography of the *Mabinogi*', *National Library of Wales Journal*, xxxii/4 (2002), 365–96.

Parry, Thomas, *A History of Welsh Literature* (Oxford, 1955).

Pearsall, D. A., *The Life of Geoffrey Chaucer* (Oxford, 1992).

Pryce, Huw, *Native Law and the Church in Medieval Wales* (Oxford, 1993).

Randall, H. J., 'Roman Period', in *A Hundred Years of Welsh Archaeology*, ed. V. E. Nash-Williams (Gloucester, 1946), 80–104.

Rees, William, *An Historical Atlas of Wales* (London, 1951).

——, *Caerphilly Castle*, 3rd edn (Caerphilly, 1974).

Richmond, I. A., *Roman Britain* (Harmondsworth, 1955).

Rivet, A. L. F. and Smith, Colin, *The Place Names of Roman Britain* (London, 1979).

Roberts, B. F., *Studies on Middle Welsh Literature* (Lewiston, 1992).

——, 'Where Were *the Four Branches of the Mabinogi* Written?', in *The Individual in Celtic Literatures*, ed. J. F. Nagy (Dublin, 2001), 61–75.

Ross, Anne, *Pagan Celtic Britain* (London, 1974).

Russell, Paul, 'Texts in Contexts: Recent Work on the Medieval Welsh Prose Tales', *Cambrian Medieval Celtic Studies*, xlv (2003), 59–72.

Sims-Williams, Patrick, 'The Riddling Treatment of the "Watchman Device" in *Branwen* and *Togail Bruidne Dá Derge*', *Studia Celtica*, xii–xiii (1977), 83–117.

——, 'The Submission of Irish Kings in Fact and Fiction', *Cambridge Medieval Celtic Studies*, xxii (1991), 31–61.

——, 'Clas Beuno and the *Four Branches of the Mabinogi*', in *150 Jahre 'Mabinogion'*, ed. Bernhard Maier and Stefan Zimmer (Tübingen, 2001), 111–27.

Sisam, Kenneth, *The Structure of 'Beowulf'* (Oxford, 1965).

Smith, J. B., 'The Kingdom of Morgannwg and the Norman Conquest of Glamorgan', *Glamorgan County History: The Middle Ages*, ed. T. B. Pugh (Cardiff, 1971), 1–43.

Southern, R. W., *The Making of the Middle Ages* (London, 1953).

——, 'From Schools to University', *The History of the University of Oxford: The Early Oxford Schools*, ed. J. I. Catto (Oxford, 1984), 1–36.

Sturzer, Ned, 'Inconsistencies and Infelicities in the Welsh Tales: Their Implications', *Studia Celtica*, xxxvii (2003), 127–42.

Taylor, A. J., *Caernarvon Castle and Town Walls* (London, 1953).

——, *Harlech Castle* (Cardiff, 1980).

Thomas, Charles, *The Early Christian Archaeology of North Britain* (London, 1971).

Thomas, R. J., *Enwau Afonydd a Nentydd Cymru* (Caerdydd, 1938).

Thompson, Stith, *Motif-Index of Folk-Literature*, 2nd edn (Copenhagen, 1955–8).

Thurneysen, Rudolph, *Die irische Helden- und Königsage* (Halle, 1921).

Tolstoy, L. N., *War and Peace* (Harmondsworth, 1957).

Valente, Roberta, 'Gwydion and Aranrhod: Crossing the Borders of Gender in *Math*', *Bulletin of the Board of Celtic Studies*, xxxv (1988), 1–9.

Vendryes, Joseph, *Lexique étymologique de l'irlandais ancien: Lettre C* (Paris, 1987).

Victory, Siân, *The Celtic Church in Wales* (London, 1977).

Wade-Evans, A. W. *The Life of St David* (London, 1923).

Walker, David, *Medieval Wales* (Cambridge, 1990).

Walsh, Paul, *Irish Men of Learning* (Dublin, 1947).

Watson, W. J., *The History of the Celtic Place-Names of Scotland* (Edinburgh, 1926).

Welsh, Andrew, 'The Traditional Narrative Motifs of *The Four Branches of the Mabinogi*', *Cambridge Medieval Celtic Studies*, xv (1988), 51–62.

——, 'Traditional Tales and the Harmonizing of Story in *Pwyll Pendeuic Dyuet*', *Cambridge Medieval Celtic Studies*, xvii (1989), 15–41.

White, Richard, 'New Light on the Origins of the Kingdom of Gwynedd', in *Astudiaethau at yr Hengerdd*, ed. Rachel Bromwich and R. Brinley Jones (Cardiff, 1978), 350–5.

Williams, Ifor, 'Nodiadau Ieithyddol', *Y Beirniad*, viii (1918–20), 256–60.

Williams, J. E. C., *Traddodiad Llenyddol Iwerddon* (Caerdydd, 1958).

Winward, Fiona, 'Some Aspects of the Women in the *Four Branches*', *Cambrian Medieval Celtic Studies*, xxxiv (1997), 77–106.

Wood, Juliette, 'The Calumniated Wife in Medieval Welsh Literature', *Cambridge Medieval Celtic Studies*, x (1985), 25–38.

Index

\